SAINTS
AT HEART
·······································

SAINTS
AT HEART

....

How Fault-Filled,
Problem-Prone, Imperfect People
Like Us
Can Be Holy

BERT GHEZZI

PARACLETE PRESS
BREWSTER, MASSACHUSETTS

2019 First Printing This Edition

Saints at Heart: How Fault-Filled, Problem-Prone, Imperfect People Like Us Can Be Holy

Copyright © 2019 by Bert Ghezzi

ISBN 978-1-64060-203-8

This book was previously published in hardcover as *The Heart of a Saint: Ten Ways to Grow Closer to God* (Frederick, MD: The Word Among Us Press, 2007), then in a second edition paperback as *Saints at Heart: How Faith-Filled, Problem-Prone, Imperfect People Like Us Can Be Holy* (Chicago, IL: Loyola Press, 2011). The present version is the third, updated edition.

Excerpts from *Conquistador Without Sword: The Life of Roque Gonzalez, SJ.* By C. J. McNaspy (Loyola University Press, 1984). Reprinted with permission of Loyola Press.

Unless otherwise noted, Scripture citations are from the New Jerusalem Bible, copyright © 1985 by Darton, Longman & Todd, Ltd., and Doubleday, a division of Bantam Doubleday Dell Publishing Group, Inc. Reprinted by permission.

Scripture citations marked (NAB) are taken from the New American Bible, revised edition © 2010, 1991, 1986, 1970 Confraternity of Christian Doctrine, Washington, D.C. and are used by permission of the copyright owner. All Rights Reserved. No part of the New American Bible may be reproduced in any form without permission in writing from the copyright owner.

Scripture citations marked (RSV) are taken from the Revised Standard Version of the Bible, copyright 1952 [2nd edition, 1971] by the Division of Christian Education of the National Council of the Churches of Christ in the United States of America. Used by permission. All rights reserved.

The Paraclete Press name and logo (dove on cross) are trademarks of Paraclete Press, Inc.

Library of Congress Cataloging-in-Publication Data

Names: Ghezzi, Bert, author. | Ghezzi, Bert. Heart of a saint.
Title: Saints at heart : how fault-filled, problem-prone, imperfect people
   like us can be holy / Bert Ghezzi ; foreword by Elizabeth Scalia.
Description: Brewster, MA : Paraclete Press, Inc., 2019. | Previously
   published: Chicago. IL : Loyola Press, 2011.
Identifiers: LCCN 2019014688 | ISBN 9781640602038 (tradepaper)
Subjects: LCSH: Christian saints—Biography. | Catholics—Biography. |
   Spiritual life—Catholic Church.
Classification: LCC BX4655.3 .G44 2019 | DDC 282.092/2 [B]—dc23
LC record available at https://lccn.loc.gov/2019014688

10 9 8 7 6 5 4 3 2 1

Published by Paraclete Press
Brewster, Massachusetts
www.paracletepress.com

Printed in the United States of America

For
George and Mary Martin

Cling to the saints,
for those who cling to them will be sanctified.
—St. Clement of Rome, *Letter to the Corinthians*

Contents

S t. Philip Neri, the great confessor and "Apostle to Rome" who was a contemporary of Sts. Ignatius Loyola and Charles Borromeo, among others, consistently urged his penitents and parishioners to read the lives of the saints: "Be often reading the lives of saints for inspiration and instruction," he is quoted as saying, adding that few were ever perfect: "What we know of the virtues of the saints is the least part of them."

It's good advice, we know, for too often we forget that the saints were not born holy; they had their human faults and frailties, just like us, which we only learn about through study, and through building relationships with them, which can sometimes happen quite by accident, or perhaps thanks to Providence and a little willingness to listen, on our part.

And how often does a word from a saint, dropped unexpectedly into our internet feed, stop us in our tracks for its pithy wisdom and lead us into further explorations of that saint's writings? I myself have had such an experience. Turned off by the sometimes treacly sentiment connected to her hagiography, I had dismissed the very idea that St. Thérèse of Lisieux might have anything to say to me until this line dropped my way, on a prayer card: "A soul in a state of grace has nothing to fear of demons, who are cowards."[1]

Whoa! It turned out the saint whose twee nickname ("The Little Flower") often made me wince was in fact a spiritual warrior who fully sniffed in powerful disdain at demons! I quickly found a copy of *The Story of a Soul* and in short order made my amends to Thérèse, offering a rose with my heartfelt respect.

This unassuming Doctor of the Church has become my go-to instructor—not on the subject of love, as one might assume (for that, I look to her startling fellow-Carmelite, Elizabeth of the Trinity)—but on *detachment*. Her "little way" teaches us how to reduce matters to a more immediate perspective, which helps us survive a crazed world or get through a particularly tough minute: "If I did not simply live from one moment to another, it would be impossible for me to be patient," she writes helpfully, "but I only look at the present, I forget the past, and I take good care not to forestall the future."[2]

Happily, I am not the first nor the last person to assume a saint has nothing to teach me. A good friend of mine, rather conservative-leaning and news-addicted, was certain Thomas Merton was some sort of radical-thinking heretic until a tweet flew by her timeline and caught her eye: "As long as I assume that the world is something I discover by turning on the radio or looking out the window, I am deceived from the start."[3]

My friend quickly got her hands-on copy of *The Seven Storey Mountain* and never looked back. For her, Merton has become a dear and daily instructor in the practice of contemplative prayer. For me, on the other hand, Merton is an insistent witness to the supernatural power of the Eucharist: "I tell you there is a power that goes forth from that Sacrament, a power of light and truth, even into the hearts of those who have heard nothing of Him and seem to be incapable of belief."[4]

Why am I sharing this? Because it's important to consider that for most saints, the pursuit of holiness softened their imperfections by broadening their understanding. Few of them are static Johnny-One-Notes with limited appeal. A priest friend of mine is fond of saying that "saints disappear into Christ," and most saints have done that so thoroughly that they cannot help but be broad in their knowledge, and thus in what we may glean from them. Once someone has fallen into the volcano of Christ, his or her lava becomes so intrinsically merged to the All-Truth, All-Light, All-Love, that when we discover them we become singed in surprising ways.

So, every saint has something to teach us, and what one saint teaches you may be completely different from the instruction another takes from the same teacher. And there are always new or lesser-known saints to discover and become intimate with. You will meet a few of them in this book.

"O St. [Name], teach me what you know," is something I pray almost daily to some spiritual ancestor or another, and when I do, I feel very much like St. Bernard of Clairvaux, who wrote: "When I think of [the saints] I feel myself inflamed by a tremendous yearning . . . a longing to enjoy their company."[5]

Most of us completely understand and identify with that feeling.

As we see, the saints themselves enjoin us to study the lives of holy people for inspiration, for guidance—and even for companionship—but mostly so that we might join their number and become part of the great "cloud of witnesses" within the Communion of Saints, whether canonized or not.

In her retreat diary, St. Bernadette Soubirous, the exceedingly humble visionary of Lourdes, nevertheless wrote with disarming confidence, "I must become a great saint. My Jesus wants it."[6]

In fact, Jesus wants all of us to pursue holiness with such confidence, such joyfulness, and such persistence that we all disappear into his Light and thus become saints.

For most of us, though, just reading the lives of holy people—helpful though it is—won't do the trick. We need some guidance in how to process the lessons we collect from their lives, adventures, and testimonials, some suggestions as to how we can not only internalize what we are learning, but practically apply it as well.

So, thank goodness that Bert Ghezzi—a great friend of the saints and author of one of my all-time favorite books, *Voices of the Saints: A Year of Readings*—has refreshed and reissued this little volume, which, despite appearances, is not just one more collection of saintly hagiographies. Rather, *Saints at Heart* might be considered a kind of "Workbook for Heaven," and like any good workbook it contains elements that are creative, enlightening, encouraging, and surprisingly fun, even when it is challenging.

Don't let that last word throw you. Bert is a gentle and good-humored teacher, and here he presents brief discussions of selected, pertinent saints chosen to constructively work on specific and valuable spiritual qualities, and then offers some excellent insight and advice before inviting us to think and to pray. His challenges are, to quote St. Benedict of Nursia's Rule, "Nothing harsh, nor burdensome . . . "[7]

Nor are they long lasting—each urge to action is time-specific and not of long duration, but all of them are meant to help us to extend our faith beyond wherever we are, and purely for the sake of working our kindness muscles, or developing a constructive habit of study and prayer through a little bit of discipline.

Personally, I appreciated being given the chance to spend a few weeks consciously doing small kindnesses for someone I like, and was surprised by its fruit; it made the light seem brighter and my own darkness was thus lessened.

That realization actually inspired me to offer daily prayers for the good of someone I *don't* like very much at all, and while I still can't say I want to become best friends with that person, in general my attitude has warmed up, and our interactions have become less chilled.

When I discussed that with my good friend Philip Neri, I imagined him responding, "Look at you! You're *sainting*!"

Such a kidder, that Neri is. But in truth, this little "Workbook" promises on what it delivers; it really does teach *How Fault-Filled, Problem-Prone, Imperfect People Like Us Can Be Holy*.

I'm planning on making this little book a gift to people whose faith I admire or want to encourage. I can't wait for those days when I see them working it—thinking, praying and doing—so I can say to them, too, "Look at you! You're *sainting*!"

—ELIZABETH SCALIA

Introduction
MATTERS OF THE HEART

Where your treasure is, there your heart will be also.
—*Matthew 6:21*

In the past twenty-five years, I have written about hundreds of saints and read about hundreds of others. I like to study their lives because I learn so much from their differences. For example, in *Saints at Heart* you will meet St. Thérèse of Lisieux and Blessed Pier Giorgio Frassati, two young saints whose lives were polar opposites. Thérèse, sick for the last few years of her life, lived a sheltered, reserved life in a convent, devoted to prayer and doing little things for others out of love. On the other hand, Pier Giorgio, vigorously healthy, lived an active life, expressing his love for Jesus in serving the poor while engaging in politics and enjoying his friends and sports. Thérèse taught me to always ask, "What is the loving thing to do now?" Pier Giorgio showed me how to live a faithful Christian life in the world with gusto. You will make similar comparisons as you read this book.

But I also like studying about saints because I learn so much from their similarities. Amid their vast diversity, one commonality stands out: they share the same heart—a heart set on loving God above all. The heart is that deep place at the core of our being where we make the choices that direct and orient our lives. At some point every one of the saints made a heartfelt decision to put God first in his or her life. St. Thérèse said it well: "I care about one thing only—to love You, my Jesus!"

This book is about drawing closer to God, and it is more about you and me than it is about the saints whose lives I describe. Holiness is not the narrowly guarded privilege of a few, but rather an abundantly available opportunity for all. "The Lord asks everything of us," said Pope Francis in *Rejoice and Be Glad,* "and in return he offers us true life, the happiness for which we were created. He wants us to be saints and not to settle for a bland and mediocre existence."[1]

Here's the point: we can become saints if we want. All we must do is choose to be holy, and the Holy Spirit will make it happen. And because making us saints is God's work, we don't have to be without problems, faults, or even sins. All of the saints, including the apostles, were sinners, just like you and me. For example, speaking about the apostles' difficulties, Pope Benedict XVI said, "This appears very consoling to me because we see that the saints did not drop out of heaven. They were men like us with problems and even with sins."[2]

In *Saints at Heart* you will read about ten ways of giving your heart more fully to God. St. Thérèse models for us the love of God, and St. Aelred, the love of others. We can advance in holiness by imitating St. Francis's ongoing conversion and by responding to God's call, as St. Katharine Drexel did. Four saints illustrate for us the key means of Christian growth: from Dorothy Day, we learn about prayer and study; from St. Angela Merici, fellowship with other Christians; from St. Roque Gonzalez, social action; and from Pope St. John Paul II, evangelization. St. Jane de Chantal and Blessed Pier Giorgio Frassati show us how to persevere joyfully through life's challenges. We will look at the lives of these women and men to see how we might respond to God's grace more willingly and generously.

You will find a set of interactive questions at the end of each chapter titled "Think, Pray, and Act." I designed them to help you reflect on the message of the saint's life and decide how you might apply it to your own. And each chapter ends with a "May you" blessing, my prayer for you that commends you to the Lord and asks for graces to help you put into practice your decision to pursue holiness.

Although an action is suggested in each chapter, you will become discouraged quickly if you attempt to add too many new practices to your routine. Better to select just one easy-to-implement, but significant, activity. I suggest that you consider starting with the questions in the chapters "Loving God" or "Prayer and Study," either of which are good places to begin advancing further on the road to holiness.

So please don't let my book get in the way of your spiritual growth by giving you too many things to do. Holiness does not come from staying busy with Christian activities. It is a matter of the heart, a matter of falling in love with God. "Let yourselves be charmed by Christ the Infinite," said Pope St. John Paul II,

who appeared among you in visible and imitable form. Let yourselves be attracted by his example, which has changed the history of the world and directed it toward an exhilarating goal. Let yourselves be loved by the Love of the Holy Spirit, who wishes to turn you away from worldly things to begin in you the life of the new self, created in God's way in righteousness and true holiness. Fall in love with Jesus Christ, to live his very life, so that our world may have life in the light of the gospel.[3]

One LOVING GOD
Saint Thérèse of Lisieux (1873–1897)

You shall love the LORD, your God, with all your heart, and
with all your soul, and with all your strength.
—*Deuteronomy 6:5 (NAB)*

We are frequently tempted to think that holiness is only
for those who can withdraw from ordinary affairs to spend
much time in prayer. That is not the case. We are all called
to be holy by living our lives with love and by bearing
witness in everything we do, wherever we find ourselves.
—POPE FRANCIS, *Rejoice and Be Glad*, 14

*If you are like me, you have great aspirations, expecting to achieve
the best life has to offer. But these expectations seem to get buried
beneath the barrage of our daily, mundane obligations. Urgent
matters always displace the important ones. However, if we set our
hearts on our goals, our everyday activities can become the means
of attaining them.*

*St. Thérèse of Lisieux claimed that at age three she had declared her
life goal: "I want to be a saint!" Perhaps her adult memory adjusted
the facts of her childhood, but there's no question that by the time
she was a teen, she had decided on holiness. So throughout her short
life she put loving God above all, and her commitment to holiness
transformed all of her daily activities into means to that end.*

*In nine years as a Carmelite nun, Thérèse loved God in the pursuit
of her ordinary duties. With God first in her thoughts, she swept the
choir loft, washed clothes, folded altar linens, escorted elderly nuns
about the convent, and cut up food for a sister who had difficulty*

eating. Unlike other great saints, she did nothing noteworthy. She did not found an order, build a hospital, or convert an aboriginal tribe. "Though the little Sister is very good," said one of her sisters, "she has never done anything worth speaking about."[1] But doing everything with love was enough to make her a saint—and a great one at that.

What does a nineteenth-century saintly nun who lived a sheltered life have to do with you and me? We live in a very different world that seems to spin faster every day. While juggling the duties of family, work, or school, navigating the freeways, and keeping up with the electronic world of email, blogs, Facebook, Twitter, and the like, we don't really have time for pursuing holiness, do we? But that's where Thérèse sets the example for us. Holiness is for everyone, not just cloistered religious. In a letter to a cousin who was about to marry, Thérèse wrote, "We all take a different road, but each one leads to the same goal. You and I must have a single aim—to grow in holiness while following the way God in his goodness has laid down for us."[2]

If we set our sights on loving God above all, then every action in the cascade of our daily activities can be an effective means to holiness. With St. Thérèse of Lisieux we should all decide to become saints and let the love of God make it happen.

When I first read an early translation of St. Thérèse's autobiography, I didn't like it very much. Her prose ran thick with over-spiritual expressions that seemed too syrupy for my taste, and as a result I found it hard to relate to her. But a few years ago I found a more contemporary version by John Beevers,[3] which appealed to me. He had stripped the book of its cloying sweetness, letting Thérèse speak in a simpler and more direct way. Beevers claims that Pauline, her older sister, ruined the original manuscript by adding adjectives, adverbs, and phrases that obscured the forcefulness of Thérèse's writing. He says that Pauline had made about seven thousand such changes,[4] some of which he fixed and so made the book more accessible to twenty-first-century readers.

Thérèse's popularity has not waned since she burst on the scene at the turn of the twentieth century. It has only increased as more people discover the breadth and depth of her spirituality. Contemporary readers of her story, like me, appreciate her as a truly modern saint, who blended the best of traditional piety with twentieth- and twenty-first-century spiritual disciplines, which she anticipated. I have in mind her forward-looking approach to Scripture, her observance of the liturgical year, her use of meditative prayer, and her refreshing disdain for self-imposed mortification.

Thérèse was born to Sts. Louis and Zélie Martin on January 2, 1873, at Alençon, a small town in northern France. Louis worked as a watchmaker and jeweler, and Zélie as a lace-maker, so the family was moderately well-to-do. The Martin's four older daughters—Marie, Pauline, Léonie, and Céline—doted on their baby sister. As a child Thérèse already showed the intelligence, joy, spunk, and strong will that marked her adult character. At the age of four, for instance, she wrote a note to one of Pauline's friends celebrating her enjoyment of the family. Pauline, she wrote, "wants me to tell you that I'm a lazy little girl, but this isn't true because I work all day long playing tricks on my poor little sisters."[5] In her autobiography, Thérèse told of a childhood experience with Léonie and Céline that revealed her innate capacity for total commitment:

One day Léonie, no doubt thinking she was too old to play with dolls, came to us both with a basket filled with their clothes, ribbons, and other odds and ends. Her own doll was on top. She said: "Here you are, darlings. Take what you want." Céline took a little bundle of silk braid. I thought for a moment, then stretched out my hand and declared "I choose everything." And without much more ado, I carried off the lot.[6]

Thérèse observed that this incident summed up her whole life. She said that later when she understood the call to holiness, she exclaimed, "My God, I choose all. I do not want to be a saint by halves."

As well-formed Catholics with a solid understanding of doctrine and practice, Louis and Zélie ran their family as a training school for their daughters. The Martins centered their life on God and the church. They worshipped at Mass on Sundays and frequently on weekdays. In the evenings they enjoyed games and storytelling and then joined together in prayer. Together, they also read and discussed Scripture and books such as Dom Prosper Gueranger's *The Liturgical Year.* Louis paid special attention to forming his youngest daughter. Often in the late afternoon he took Thérèse for walks to nearby churches, where at prayer before the tabernacle she acquired a devotion to Jesus in the Eucharist. As an adult she recalled having accompanied her father on fishing trips, during which she accidentally stumbled upon meditative prayer. "Sometimes I tried to fish with my own little rod," she wrote, "but I preferred to sit amidst the grass and flowers. I thought deeply then and, although I was quite ignorant about meditation, my soul did plunge into a state of real prayer."[7] Thus, the Martin family life planted the seeds of holiness in Thérèse.

Zélie died of cancer in 1877, bringing an end to Thérèse's bright early childhood. She comforted herself by adopting Pauline as her "little Mother." Louis moved the family to Lisieux in order to be near the supportive family of Zélie's brother. During these difficult transitions, Thérèse became melancholy and began to suffer a variety of nervous ailments, which lasted for several years.

When Thérèse was nine, Pauline entered the Carmelite convent at Lisieux. For several months Thérèse reacted to the loss of her second mother with headaches, insomnia, hypersensitivity, and bouts of weeping. Visits to Pauline failed to console her. Temporary relief came one day when her sisters knelt before a statue of Mary and asked her to intercede for Thérèse's healing. She reported in her autobiography that Mary smiled at her through the statue and delivered her from her pain.[8] But the ailments soon returned. Even the joy Thérèse experienced at her first Communion and Confirmation did not dispel them. Extreme sensitivity, loneliness, and mind-numbing attacks of scruples continued to plague her.

A life-changing event occurred on Christmas morning in 1886 that finally brought Thérèse deliverance from these terrible problems. She had prayed for a miracle to bring her peace, freedom, and strength to resist her hypersensitivity. And just after midnight Mass she received it. "Jesus, the Child then only an hour old," she said,

> flooded the darkness of my soul with torrents of light. By becoming weak and frail for me, He gave me strength and courage. He clothed me with His weapons, and from that blessed night I was unconquerable. I went from victory to victory and began to run as a giant.[9]

At home after Mass, Thérèse overheard her father snap that he was glad it was the last time they would have to endure the family ritual of surprising her with gifts. She handled this emotionally fraught episode with unusual composure, which assured her that the miracle was genuine.

Thérèse regarded this event as closing her childhood and opening her life as an adult. Years later she recalled how the miracle gave her a heart for the conversion of sinners:

> Jesus . . . accomplished in an instant what I had been unable to do in ten years. Like the apostles, we could say: "Master, I have toiled all the night, and caught nothing." Jesus was more merciful to me than to His disciples. He Himself took the net, cast it, and drew it up full of fishes. He made me a fisher of men. I longed to work for the conversion of sinners with a passion I'd never felt before. Love filled my heart, I forgot myself and henceforth I was happy.[10]

This experience launched Thérèse's lifelong practice of interceding for serious wrongdoers.

In her fourteenth year, Thérèse heard God calling her to enter the Carmelite convent at Lisieux—and she became determined to do so by Christmas 1887, just before her fifteenth birthday. Her father gave his permission, but the superior at Carmel refused to consider her for admission until she was at least sixteen. Thérèse and her father appealed to the local bishop, but he sided with the superior, telling her that she was too young to become a nun. "I've longed to give myself to God ever since I was three,"[11] objected Thérèse, but the bishop held his ground.

Thérèse was disappointed but not deterred. On a pilgrimage to Rome a few weeks later, she boldly asked Pope Leo XIII at a papal audience to let her enter Carmel at fifteen. The pope told her to obey the local authorities. "You will enter," he said, "if God wills."[12]

Deeply distressed but at peace beneath the surface of her feelings, Thérèse entrusted to Jesus her campaign to become a Carmelite. But he seemed to ignore her request. Thérèse had often imagined herself as a little ball that the Child Jesus could play with and treat any way he wanted. "I longed to amuse the little Jesus and offer myself to his childish whims." When the pope denied her at Rome, she felt as though Jesus had pierced his toy to see what was inside, and then let it drop and went to sleep.[13]

However, Thérèse did not stop expecting God to intervene on her behalf. And finally the obstacles began to fall away. Just after Christmas, perhaps influenced by his vicar-general, who had promised Thérèse that he would intercede for her, the bishop changed his mind and gave permission for her to enter Carmel immediately. But the Carmelite superior tested Thérèse's endurance further by holding off her admission until after Easter 1888.

On April 9, 1888, Thérèse Martin disappeared into the Carmel at Lisieux and as Sister Thérèse of the Child Jesus began her nine undistinguished years as a nun. She served as assistant novice master for three years, but that was the only office she held in the Carmelite community. Her charism was simply loving God above all. "Now I wish for only one thing," she once wrote, "to love Jesus unto folly!"[14]

Thérèse did not set out to develop a method for holiness. If she had foreseen that one day Pope John Paul II would declare her a Doctor of the Church, she would have wondered why and may even have laughed at the apparent incongruity of the idea. She would have been uncomfortable to be universally recognized as a spiritual guide. "Jesus has no need of books or Doctors of the Church to guide souls," she wrote. He, the Doctor of doctors,

> can teach without words. I have never heard Him speak, but I know that He is within me. He guides and inspires me every moment of the day. Just when I need it, a new light shines on my problems. This happens not so much during my hours of prayer as when I'm busy with my daily work.[15]

AN IMMEASURABLE LOVE
Thomas à Kempis (c. 1380–1471)

Loving God above all is at the heart of Thomas à Kempis's teaching in The Imitation of Christ.

O my Lord God, most faithful Lover, when You come into my heart, all within me rejoices. You are my glory and the joy of my heart, my hope and my whole refuge in all my troubles. . . .

Love knows no measure, but is fervent without measure. It feels no burdens; it regards no labor; it desires more than it can obtain. It complains of no impossibility, for it thinks all things that can be done for its Beloved are possible and lawful. . . .

He who is thus a spiritual lover knows well what that voice means which says: "You, Lord God, are my whole love and my desire. You are all mine, and I all Yours. Dissolve my heart into Your love so that I may know how sweet it is to serve You and how joyful it is to praise You, and to be as though I were all melded into Your love. Oh, I am urged on by love and go far above myself because of the great fervor I feel through your unspeakable goodness. I shall sing to You the song of love; I shall follow You, my Beloved, in flights of thought wherever You go, and my soul will never be weary in praising You with the joyful songs of spiritual love that I will sing to you. I will love You more than myself, and will not love myself except for You; and I shall love others in You and for You, as the law of love which You give commands."

—Thomas à Kempis, *The Imitation of Christ,* trans. Richard Whitford, ed. Harold Gardiner (New York: Image Books, 1989), 109–11.

As a teen, Thérèse had devoured *The Imitation of Christ* and the works of St. Teresa of Avila, St. John of the Cross, and many other spiritual writers. However, in the sunset of her life, she grew tired of spiritual treatises that said perfection was hard to attain. Once she said, "I shut the learned book which is giving me a headache and drying up my heart, and I open the holy Scriptures. Then everything seems clear; one word opens up infinite horizons, perfection seems easy. I see that it is sufficient to abandon myself like a child in God's arms."[16] Apparently Thérèse enjoyed a form of Scripture meditation that twenty-first-century Catholics still find attractive and practical.

Those of us who have difficulties with prayer can appreciate Thérèse's candid admission that she often fell asleep while meditating. Since I ocasionally nod off during my morning prayer, I am heartened by her observation that God, like any good parent, loves his children dearly whether they are asleep or awake.[17] Thérèse also endured long stretches of dryness, but instead of worrying about it, she delighted in it. She envisioned that in times of spiritual aridity, Jesus was "asleep in her little boat." Instead of shaking him awake as others did, she let him sleep peacefully, as she thought that he must be wearied by all he has to do for us. Imagining that her dryness afforded Jesus much-needed rest pleased her.[18] Without thinking critically about the theological accuracy of her perspective, I plan to imitate her approach the next time my prayer gets dry.

Thérèse did not believe in using penitential practices except the fasting required in the Carmelite rule. She especially advised against using "instruments of penance" to discipline the body. She argued that Jesus said his yoke was easy and his burden light. He did not tell us to burden ourselves with extra weight.[19] I find her view comforting, because I, like many contemporaries, believe that enough suffering comes our way daily that we don't need to impose additional bodily pain on ourselves. Thérèse said that her real penance was breaking her self-love by serving others when she did not feel like it and doing little kindnesses that went unnoticed.

While Thérèse used spiritual disciplines, she did not view them as causes of perfection. "Holiness," she said, "does not consist of any one particular method of spirituality: it is a disposition of heart which makes us small and humble within the arms of God, aware of our weakness but almost rashly confident in His fatherly goodness."[20] Committed from childhood to become a saint, she had always sought perfection. But toward the end of her life, she realized that the harder she ran after it, the further away it seemed to be. She came to embrace her imperfections and even to relish them. She once assured a novice at Carmel not to worry about her faults because God was blind to arithmetic. "Were He clear-sighted enough to see all our sins, if He were good enough at figures to be able to total up their number, He would send us straight back to our nothingness. But His love for us makes Him blind."[21]

Thérèse was convinced that God had called her to be a saint. However, when she compared herself to the saints, she felt like a grain of sand in the presence of mountains reaching into the clouds. She decided that God knew of her littleness and would provide her a "little way" to get to heaven. Observing that in some mansions you could take an elevator instead of climbing stairs, Thérèse determined to find an elevator that would carry her to Jesus, "because I was far too small to climb the stairs of perfection." She searched the Bible and found her elevator in Proverbs 9:4, "Whosoever is a little one, let him come to me," and Isaiah 66:12–13, "You shall be carried at the breasts and upon the knees." The arms of Jesus would be the elevator that would carry her to heaven. "And so there is no need for me to grow up," she said. "In fact just the opposite: I must stay little and become less and less."[22]

Total reliance on Jesus constituted the heart of Thérèse's "little way." Then, resting comfortably in his arms, anyone could become holy by doing ordinary things for love. "The most trivial act," she said,

> one that no one knows about, provided it is inspired by love, is often of greater worth than the greatest achievement. It is not the value or even the apparent holiness of deeds which counts, but only the love put into them. And no one can say that he cannot do these little things for God, for everyone is capable of them.[23]

Thérèse herself aspired to achieve great things for love of God. She wished she could be a missionary who evangelized the whole world. She also wanted to be a martyr who suffered every torment endured by those who had given their life for Christ. But she decided that she was too little and too weak for such greatness. Instead of settling for a lesser vocation, she chose a calling even higher than foreign missions or martyrdom. She chose to do everything with love and so become a channel of grace for others. "I care now about one thing only," she wrote, "to love You, my Jesus! . . . The only way I can prove my love is by scattering flowers and these flowers are every little sacrifice, every glance and word, and the doing of the least of actions for love."[24] She believed that Christ would use the graces released by her little sacrifices to strengthen the church and bring relief to those who suffered.

DOING LITTLE THINGS FOR GOD

God shows his love . . . with simple, tender acts of charity. What does [Jesus] say? He doesn't say, "I think God is like this. I have understood God's love." No, no. "I made God's love small." He expressed God's love concretely on a small scale by feeding someone who was hungry, giving the thirsty something to drink, visiting a prisoner or someone who is ill. Therefore, there is no need for grand speeches about love, but there is a need for men and women who know how to do these little things for Jesus, for the Father.

—POPE FRANCIS, Homily, June 8, 2018

Thérèse wrote this summary of her life's mission shortly before her death. She contracted tuberculosis during Holy Week in 1896. For the next year and a half she endured severe physical pain and spiritual agony. She died on September 30, 1897, a nun who had been enclosed for nine years in an obscure Carmelite convent. But popular devotion to Thérèse spread rapidly soon after her death, due both to the publication and widespread circulation of her autobiography and to grace.

So many thousands testified to miracles won through her intercession that authorities in the Vatican hastened her canonization. Pope Pius XI declared her a saint in 1925. And from her home in heaven, she achieved one of her deepest longings. In 1927 the pope declared her, along with St. Francis Xavier, a principal patron of all missionaries.

Think, Pray, and Act

Few of us will become great missionaries or martyrs. But all of us can embrace the higher calling of loving God above all and imitating Thérèse's practice of letting that love direct all of our actions. Then our lives, too, will become channels of grace, supporting others on their journey to God.

Take stock of your life to determine how you might adopt the principles of St. Thérèse's "little way." Use the following questions to help you consider how to love God more and do even the most trivial things for love.

Think

- How much do I love God? How would I describe my relationship with him?

- How often do I perform little acts of kindness without expecting any thanks or notice?

Pray

Set aside a half hour of quiet prayer and reflect on the following questions.

- Do I put God first in my life? If not, what occupies first place in my mind and heart?

- What difference would it make for my life if I decided that I wanted to become a saint?

Act

- What one action could I take that would increase my love for God?

✶ Select one person in your set of closest relationships. For two weeks, pray for that person daily and perform small acts of service for him or her each day. At the end of the two weeks, take time to reflect on what you learned.

May you hear God's call to you with clarity and without confusion. And may you choose to be a saint and find the grace to pursue holiness.

Two LOVING OTHERS
SAINT AELRED OF RIEVAULX (1110–1167)

Love one another, as I have loved you. No one can have
greater love than to lay down his life for his friends.
—*John 15:12–13*

The proof of the pudding is in the eating.
—CERVANTES, *Don Quixote*

True faith is one that makes us more charitable, more
merciful, more honest and more humane. It moves
our hearts to love everyone without counting the cost,
without distinction and without preference. It makes
us see the other not as an enemy to be overcome, but a
brother or sister to be loved, served and helped.
—POPE FRANCIS, Address to the Vincentians, October 14, 2017

*To paraphrase an ancient proverb, the proof of the Christian life is
in the living. Surveying our church-related activities may persuade
us that we are doing okay. We may be attending Sunday worship,
putting some money in the collection, spending time in personal
prayer each day, saying grace before and after meals, attending a
Bible study, or volunteering in a ministry.*

*But the real test of our Christianity looks behind these pursuits
and goes deeper. To assess how well we are doing we must ask a
question that comes with the highest authority: Am I loving others
as Jesus commanded? That question embraces many people: Am
I loving my family? My neighbors? My friends? My companions
at church? My coworkers or fellow students? My enemies? (Don't
pretend that you don't have any—how about the last guy who cut*

you off in traffic?) And the question involves many behaviors: Am I being kind? Putting up with people's quirks? Forgiving offenses? Giving encouragement? Supplying needs? If we aren't loving others in these ways and think we are loving God, we are fooling ourselves. "No one who fails to love the brother whom he can see," said St. John, "can love God whom he has not seen" (1 John 4:20).

All saints model the love of others for us. Even the solitaries in the desert maintained healthy relationships. But for me, St. Aelred of Rievaulx, a twelfth-century abbot, stands out as an exemplar of Christian charity and friendship. When I encountered him a decade ago while researching a book on the saints, I fell in love with him. My four sons—John, Paul, Stephen, and Peter—all rejoice that I named them before I met Aelred (just as my three daughters celebrate that they were born before I met St. Lutgarde, another twelfth-century favorite of mine). Although Aelred lived and wrote nearly nine hundred years ago, under circumstances that were very different from ours, his example and his teaching on charity and friendship still seem fresh today.

Aelred was born in 1110, to a priest and his wife at Hexam in northern England. (A married clergy was still allowed then, but the practice was on its way out.) Home-schooled by a local priest and an uncle, Aelred received a solid education, including Latin language and literature. His aristocratic family had ties to the kings of England and Scotland. Those relationships may account for an opportunity that came to him when he was fifteen. He was sent to live in the court of King St. David I of Scotland (c. 1085–1153), the son of St. Margaret (1045–1093). There Aelred's innate friendliness charmed everyone, and he formed lifelong friendships with Henry, the heir to the throne, with the king's stepsons Simon and Waldef, and with King David himself.

Aelred lived for nine years in the Scottish court. The king recognized his gifts and appointed him in his late teens as a steward over household details, including the kitchen. Aelred absorbed the courtly culture, acquiring diplomatic skills that would serve him well in later life. However, in his early twenties he grew increasingly discouraged with the shallowness of his associations at court. He realized that he had many gifts, but did not know how he was supposed to use them. So, he worried especially over his lack of a clear vocation.[1]

In 1134, in this conflicted state of mind, Aelred went on a mission for the king to Archbishop Thurston of York. On his return he stayed with Walter Espec at his castle at Helmsley. Two years before, Archbishop Thurston and Espec, a powerful northern lord, had founded the Cistercian monastery of Rievaulx in the Yorkshire forest near the castle. St. Bernard (c. 1090–1153) had sent a small contingency of monks from Clairvaux in Burgundy to start the community.[2] Conversations about the monastery piqued Aelred's curiosity, so he visited Rievaulx and was moved by the fervor of the monks. Instead of heading home the next day as planned, he headed for Rievaulx and presented himself for membership in the community. He believed he had found the calling that would give him the life direction for which he had longed.

Don't imagine early Rievaulx as a set of elaborate buildings fabricated of stone, mahogany panels, and bronze fixtures. Picture rather a cluster of rough-hewn huts on hardscrabble land in the Yorkshire wilds. Picture, too, how difficult it must have been for the refined, slightly built aristocrat to adjust to the heavy work of cultivating the fields. Although he cheerfully joined the worship and work of his brothers, demons of confusion still tormented the young monk. To overcome temptations and to focus his spirit on his calling, Aelred often prayed while immersed in a pool of icy water.[3] Devotees of the twenty-first-century Celtic revival have conveniently overlooked that frigid practice, which was common among twelfth-century monks. This and other severe mortifications weakened Aelred's already frail body and contributed to the illnesses that plagued him in later life.

Aelred's considerable gifts did not go unnoticed. The abbot confided in him and consulted him on pastoral matters. In 1142 he placed Aelred on a team sent to Rome to protest the choice of William Fitzherbert as Archbishop of York. His diplomatic skills contributed to the success of the intervention, but the real significance of the Rome visit occurred on the trek home. Aelred seized the chance to visit Clairvaux, where he met and became a friend of Bernard, who took note of his thoughtfulness and potential as a writer. Upon Aelred's return to Rievaulx, the abbot appointed him master of novices, an office he pursued with obvious affection and compassion for his younger brothers. He formed them with talks that summed up what he had learned about living as a monk. He kept his notes, which soon became a valuable resource for his writing. In 1143 Bernard sent a letter to Aelred directing him to write a book of his reflections on community life under the title *The Mirror of Charity*. Aelred objected that he had come from the kitchen, not the schools, but Bernard insisted that his stewardship over earthly food was the training for his calling to provide spiritual food in books.[4]

At Bernard's request, in *The Mirror of Charity* Aelred defended the strict observance of fasting and mortification required of Cistercian monks, many of whom felt they could not endure its burden. Although the book is a treatise about monastic discipline, it still contains timeless practical wisdom for all Christians. In the mirror of Scripture, says Aelred, we can see Christ's generous love of God that drove him to the Cross. In that same mirror we can also behold our sinfulness that we can renounce by loving

God generously.[5] When we are freed from dependence on sin, we are enabled to love our neighbors well. Some people, Aelred says, we will love easily, because we are attracted to them, but in these cases, we must guard against loving them either in excess or for selfish motives. And we must choose by force of will and God's grace to love others we don't like and treat them kindly.[6] Just as the monastery was a school of love for Aelred, the church community can be a school of love for us.

In 1143, the abbot sent Aelred to found the monastery of St. Laurence, at Revesby, near York, one of Rievaulx's earliest daughter houses. He spent four years there as abbot, developing his pastoral skills. Then in 1147 he returned to Rievaulx as abbot, where he served his brothers well for twenty years.

Aelred ruled the men of Rievaulx with great gentleness. His earlier experience as novice master made him compassionate toward the monks and sensitive to the challenges of their day-to-day lives. His natural winsomeness attracted men to the community and assured all of his care for them. Once he wrote a Pastoral Prayer to keep him focused on exercising his leadership with Christlike humility. "You know my heart, Lord," he wrote,

> and that whatsoever you have given to me, your servant, I desire to offer wholly to [my brothers] and to consume it all in their service. . . . My senses and my speech, my leisure and my labor, my acts and my thoughts, my good fortune and bad, my health and sickness, my life and death, all my stock in the world, may it by used up in their interest for whom you did not refuse to be consumed yourself. . . . Grant to me, Lord, by your indescribable grace to bear their infirmities with patient, tender, helpful compassion. May I learn by the teaching of your Spirit to console the sorrowful, to strengthen the faint-hearted, to put the fallen on their

feet, to calm the restless, to cherish the sick, conforming myself to each one's character and capacity. . . . You know, sweet Lord, how much I love them and how my heart goes out to them in tenderest affection, . . . that I yearn rather to help them in charity than to rule them.[7]

Aelred's prayer remains evergreen, one that all leaders—dads, moms, pastors, bosses, politicians—should pray daily.

THE SECRET OF LOVE

The Lord, if you let him teach you, will show you how to make tenderness and affection even more beautiful. He will guide your hearts to "love without being possessive", to love others without trying to own them but letting them be free. Because love is free! . . . The Lord, if you listen to his voice, will reveal to you the secret of love. It is *caring for* others, respecting them, protecting them and waiting for them. This is putting tenderness and love into action.

—POPE FRANCIS, Homily to Youth, April 24, 2016

As abbot, Aelred behaved as he prayed he would. He tempered the harshness of his monks' routines by encouraging them to develop relationships and allowing them to express signs of affection, such as manly hugs. Unlike other medieval abbots, who discharged monks for minor infractions of the rule, Aelred did not dismiss a single monk in his twenty years as abbot.[8] He governed with kindness, not laxity, and always found a way to help a troubled or troublesome brother. He regarded Rievaulx as a "community of love" and described it in a letter to his sister: "As I was walking round the cloisters, all the brothers sat together . . . and in the whole of that throng I could not find one whom I did not love, and by whom I was not loved."[9]

DAILY KINDNESSES
Saint John Baptist de la Salle (1651–1719)

The founder of the Christian Brothers urges us to be kind,
especially to people we do not like.

Adapt yourself with gracious and charitable compliance to all your neighbor's weaknesses. In particular, make a rule to hide your feelings in many inconsequential matters. Give up all bitterness toward your neighbor, no matter what. And be convinced that your neighbor is in everything better than you. This will not be difficult if you keep even a little aware of yourself. It will give you the ability to overcome your feelings of resentment.

Each day look for every possible opportunity to do a kindness for those you do not like. After examining yourself on this matter every morning, decide what you are going to do, and do it faithfully with kindness and humility.

Be sure to be warmly affable toward everyone. Speak to and answer everyone with very great gentleness and deference. Keep in mind the way the Lord spoke and replied to others even when he was most harshly treated. Never comment on the faults or the behavior of your neighbors. When others speak of them, put a good interpretation on their actions. If you cannot, say nothing at all.

In short, decide never to speak of the failings of others nor to reprimand them, no matter how serious they seem to you. When you see someone fall into some fault, call to mind the gospel saying, "You can see the splinter in your brother's eye, but `you cannot see the beam in your own." (See Matthew 7:3.)

—*The Letters of John Baptist de La Salle,* trans. Colman Molloy (Romeoville, IL: Lasallian Publications, 1988), letter 105, 219.

Under Aelred's wise leadership, Rievaulx grew to include 150 choir monks and five hundred brothers, who worked the fields and tended sheep. Aelred also supervised the establishment of numerous daughter houses, which he tried to visit annually. His achievements are all the more remarkable because he suffered constantly from kidney stones, dysentery, and arthritis. On one occasion, his biographer, Walter Daniel, came upon him bent over before the fireplace "like a leaf of parchment," trying to alleviate his pain.[10] After 1157 Aelred became so ill that he had to be excused from the monastery's common activities. He had a little cell constructed near the infirmary, where he stayed most of the time. From his bed he conducted the abbey's affairs and continued his care for his brothers. Twenty or thirty monks at a time crowded around him, some lying across his bed, listening to his teaching and chatting with him about all sorts of things.[11]

In 1164 Aelred resumed writing the book *Spiritual Friendship*, which he had begun around 1143 when he was abbot at Revesby. As a youth he had discovered Cicero's treatise on friendship, and the Roman orator's reflections had helped him sort out his boyish affections. Now in this book he adapted Cicero's teaching by supporting it with Scripture. All human friendships, he said, had their source in God, who created human beings to share his love by loving him and each other.[12] Paraphrasing St. John, he said, "He who abides in friendship abides in God, and God in him."[13] But since friendship was a special form of love between two sinful people, Aelred repeated the cautions he had placed in *The Mirror of Charity*. Friendship entered for the wrong reasons, such as for vice or gain, deteriorated into a perverse love that Aelred called "cupidity," which must be avoided.

However, Aelred said that when we take care to form a good friendship, one free of sin's perversions, we will enjoy wonderful benefits:

> It is no small consolation in this life to have someone you can unite with you in an intimate affection and the embrace of a holy love. Someone in whom your spirit can rest, to whom you can pour out your soul, to whose pleasant exchanges, as to soothing songs, you can fly in sorrow. To the dear breast of whose friendship, amidst the many troubles of the world, you can safely retire. A person who can shed tears with you in your worries, be happy with you when things go well, search out with you the answers to your problems, whom with the ties of charity you can lead into the depths of your heart. A person who, though absent in body, is yet present in spirit, where heart to heart you can talk to him, where the sweetness of the Spirit flows between you, where you so join yourself and cleave to him that soul mingles with soul and two become one.
>
> And so praying to Christ for your friend, and longing to be heard by Christ for your friend's sake, you reach out with devotion and desire to Christ himself. And suddenly and insensibly, as though touched by the gentleness of Christ close at hand, you begin to taste how sweet he is and to feel how lovely he is. Thus from that holy love with which you embrace your friend, you rise to that love by which you embrace Christ.[14]

Aelred wrote these words sometime in the year before his death on January 12, 1167. We can easily apply them as a eulogy to a saint who lived entirely for love and friendship.

Aelred's life and message offer a medicine for our endemic social and spiritual ailments. He developed his teaching for twelfth-century monks who lived apart from the world, but it translates well to the experience of twenty-first-century laypeople who live smack in its midst. His take on Christian love and friendship, if we apply it, will cure our loneliness, our selfishness, and our shallow and sometimes sinful relationships.

Think, Pray, and Act

Take stock of your life to determine how you might adopt St. Aelred's teaching on love and friendship. Use the following questions to help you consider how to love others more.

Think

℣ What is the status of the significant relationships in my life? What word would I use to describe them? Good? Just Okay? Indifferent? Dysfunctional? Bad?

℣ Make a list of the important relationships in your life, such as with your spouse, children, parents, close relatives, roommates, neighbors, parishioners, coworkers, or friends. Use one of the above words to characterize each relationship and explain why you chose that particular word.

Pray

℣ Spend a quiet half hour reflecting on Colossians 3:1–17. Read the selection several times. Which verse seems to speak most directly to you about your way of relating to others?

℣ Ask the Holy Spirit to show you a way to respond to your conclusions about the message of Colossians 3:1–17 and the state of your relationships.

Act

→ Select one person in your set of relationships with whom you have daily contact. For the next two weeks, pray each day for that person and perform little acts of kindness for him or her. At the end of the period, take some time to reflect on what the experience taught you about your relationships. (Yes, this is the same assignment you had on the last chapter, but it will help you form the habit of loving others more.)

May you always give love to all freely and affectionately. May you have the wisdom to form good and permanent friendships. And may you shape your behavior by always asking, "What is the loving thing to do now?"

Three CONVERSION
Saint Francis of Assisi (1182–1226)

And we, who with unveiled faces all reflect the Lord's glory, are being transformed into his likeness with ever-increasing glory, which comes from the Lord, who is the Spirit.
—*2 Corinthians 3:18 (NIV)*

I invite all Christians, everywhere, at this very moment, to a renewed personal encounter with Jesus Christ, or at least an openness to letting him encounter them; I ask all of you to do this unfailingly each day.
—Pope Francis, *The Joy of the Gospel*, 3.

Francis would not suddenly become perfect, but he was to pass gradually from the flesh to the spirit.
—Thomas of Celano

For most of us, the word "conversion" brings to mind a sudden change of heart. We instantly recall, for example, the dramatic turnaround of Saul of Tarsus, when Christ appeared to him on the road to Damascus. Or we may think of the last-minute, fearful choices of soldiers under fire or of a curmudgeonly uncle on his deathbed. But most Christian conversions are neither sudden, nor dramatic, nor last-minute, nor fear-driven. Most often, we make our turnings gradually, struggling for years to break away from unworthy behaviors and to give ourselves more fully to God.

St. Francis of Assisi is a case in point. We may imagine that he had a sudden conversion when he first kissed a leper, heard Jesus speak to him from the cross at San Damiano, or repudiated his father and renounced his inheritance. For sure, each of these and other events played a significant part in his conversion, but none of them alone struck him as a "Damascus Road" experience. Rather they were the pieces in the puzzle that he contemplated as he tried to conform his worldly longings to God's will for his life. Francis's transformation from Assisi's reveler to Assisi's saint took nearly a decade, from about 1200 to 1208.

Like St. Francis, most of us have not had one, overarching Damascus Road conversion. We have had many smaller conversions, each significant in the process of our transformation, but no single experience clinching it. And we may still be puzzling over how we are to conform our comfortable behaviors to the uncomfortable standard of holiness that God invites us to embrace. St. Francis showed us how. Once he understood what the Lord wanted, he hurried to do it. We would do well to imitate him.

St. Francis was born in Assisi, Italy, in 1182. His father, Pietro di Bernardone, was a prosperous textile merchant and an upwardly mobile member of the middle class. Francis grew up at a time when Italy boiled with wars, town versus town, middle classes against nobles, and emperors versus popes. Troubadours toured the land, celebrating the ideals of chivalry and knighthood. Young Francis idolized the legendary King Arthur and his Knights of the Round Table. And he aspired to become a knight himself.

In his late teens Francis learned his father's trade well and became skilled at buying and selling cloth. He conducted business cautiously, but spent his considerable wealth carelessly.[1] Affable and generous to a fault, Francis attracted the young people of Assisi like pins to a magnet. He threw lavish banquets and drinking parties for them. Late at night, full of wine and good humor, he and his buddies paraded boisterously along Assisi's narrow streets, joking, shouting, and singing troubadour songs gleefully off-key. So he earned a well-deserved reputation as ringleader of the town's youthful revelers. Some of the partygoers may have engaged in bad behavior, but Francis maintained a high moral standard, respected women, was well mannered, and refused to tolerate offensive conversations.[2] As a counterpoint to his carousing and a prophetic clue to his future, even as a teen, Francis always gave generously to the poor. His youthful almsgiving nudged him toward conversion.

Francis's prideful conviction that he would attain knighthood after a successful battle occasioned the early stages of his transformation. With high hopes, in 1202 he joined in Assisi's war against its neighbor Perugia. No knightly honor for Francis this time, as Perugia won the war and imprisoned many of Assisi's warriors, including Francis. For a year he joyfully endured the squalor of the jail, much to the disgruntlement of his fellow prisoners. "Why should I be miserable?" he said. "Someday I'm going to be a famous saint."[3] Was Francis joking to entertain his prison mates, or was the desire to serve God already taking root in his heart? My guess is that the answer to both questions is yes, and that the joke announced an aspiration that was beginning to take root in him.

Upon his release, Francis returned to Assisi, where he resumed his previous lifestyle. But he soon fell gravely ill and spent most of 1204 bedridden. The sickness gave him plenty of time to think, and he began to question the things he valued. One day he ventured outside to view the beauty of the fields, vineyards, and mountains that had always thrilled him. But he discovered that he no longer took much delight in them.[4] He wondered about the change that was coming over him and about his newfound disregard for things he had previously loved and pursued. He felt he was leaving his former life behind, but did not yet know where he was headed.

A revived passion for war and chivalry soon pushed those thoughts to the back of Francis's mind. In the spring of 1205, he heard that a local knight was headed to Apulia to join an army that was defending the pope. The idea of accompanying the warrior inflamed his imagination. One night he dreamed of a palace that held an armory of weapons and a beautiful bride.[5] The dream's promise persuaded him that he might emerge from the war honored as a knight. With unbridled enthusiasm he furnished himself with the best armor and weaponry. Before he left Assisi, however, moved by his characteristic compassion, Francis traded his top-of-the-line gear with a poor knight for the latter's shabby equipment.

Francis never made it to Apulia. On the way he fell ill at Spoleto. There he had another dream that corrected his misinterpretation of the earlier vision. "Francis, where are you going?" asked a voice.

"To Apulia, to fight," he said.

"Who can benefit you more, the servant or the Lord?" asked the voice.

"The Lord," said Francis.

"Why then are you seeking the servant in place of the Lord?"

Francis, recognizing the speaker, said, "Lord, what do you want me to do?"

"Go back to your place of birth," said the Lord, "for through me your vision will have a spiritual fulfillment."[6] So, Francis returned to Assisi, now more convinced that God was unfolding a new purpose for him, but he did not yet see clearly what it was.

Back at home, opposing impulses tugged at Francis. He wanted to explore God's direction for him, but he could not avoid his old friends, who still expected him to be the life of their parties. One evening, however, after a banquet he had sponsored, Francis separated himself from the crowd that sang through Assisi's streets. As he stood in a quiet square, God touched him so palpably that he lost all self-awareness. Later he said that the Lord's visitation so stripped him of all other feelings that he could have been chopped up limb by limb and would not have felt it.[7] Francis remained in this heavenly state until a friend, who found him and noticed his faraway look, teased him.

"Francis," he taunted, "are you dreaming of your honeymoon?"

"Yes," said Francis. "I am thinking of getting married. But the bride I am going to take is nobler, richer, and fairer than any woman you know."[8]

Other friends who had arrived on the scene laughed at his boast. Later, when Francis reflected on the event, he grew angry with himself for not clearly breaking with his former ways. From that time, he determined to think less of himself and pursue God more aggressively.

Francis found a cave outside of town and began to go there each day to pray. He wanted to serve the Lord, whom he was coming to know better. So he wrestled with God, begging for answers to his questions: *Lord, what do you want me to do? Where do you want me to go? What did my dream about the weapons mean? Who is the bride reserved for me?* Even though answers did not come clearly, Francis regarded the new intimacy he found with God as having discovered a treasure.

Francis probably had an inkling that his bride-to-be was Lady Poverty, as he would name her later. For when he was not praying, Francis now spent even more time serving the poor. He had always loved poor people, but believed he could never truly appreciate their poverty until he experienced for himself what it was like to live as a beggar. He was too well known in Assisi to experiment with begging, so he took advantage of a pilgrimage to Rome to assume the role of a beggar for a day. He borrowed the rags of a homeless man and blended in with the poor outside St. Peter's, sharing their squalor, eating their scraps, and feeling their shame. He returned to Assisi the next day, more comfortable with the idea of living in poverty and somewhat prepared to embrace his "lady."

Francis continued his regimen of seeking God's will at the cave, and one day he sensed the Lord reveal the hint of an answer. In his spirit he heard God say,

> Francis! If you want to know my will, you must despise everything that you have loved and desired in the flesh. When you do this, all that now seems sweet and lovely to you will become bitter and intolerable, but all that you used to abhor will turn into great sweetness and immeasurable joy.[9]

To Francis, this message seemed to convey a course of action that would lead him to his purpose, if he could unravel the riddle of the sweet to bitter and the bitter to sweet. He affirmed his decision to renounce his worldly wants and attachments. And he waited for God to show him the meaning of the conundrum.

MEETING GOD IN ORDINARY CIRCUMSTANCES

The Lord reveals himself to us not in an extraordinary or impressive way, but in the everyday circumstances of our life. There we must discover the Lord; and there he reveals himself, makes his love felt in our heart; and there—with this dialogue with him in the everyday circumstances of life—he changes our heart.

—POPE FRANCIS, Angelus, January 22, 2017

He did not have long to wait. Soon after hearing the Lord, while riding on horseback, he suddenly came upon a leper. Nothing had ever repulsed Francis more than the rotting flesh and stench of a leprous person. When he saw lepers on the road, he usually turned and fled. If he wanted to give them alms, he had someone deliver it for him. On this occasion, too, he was about to run, but then he remembered the thrust of the Lord's message, that what "you used to abhor will turn into great sweetness and immeasurable joy." As Pope Francis says, "The Lord reveals himself to us not in an extraordinary or impressive way, but in the everyday circumstances of our life."

Now the Lord's prescribed course of action became clear. He dismounted and forced himself to approach the leper. The diseased man's disgusting odor triggered his reaction to vomit, but he gulped it back. He gave some money to the leper, and with a mighty act of will kissed him.

To Francis's great joy, the Lord's prophetic promise came true. A generous sense of peace flooded his being. And his faithful response had occasioned a key moment in his transformation. He remembered it in his Testament, which he wrote twenty years later, just before he died:

> When I was in sin, the sight of lepers nauseated me beyond measure; but then God himself led me into their company, and I had pity on them. When I had once become acquainted with them, what had previously nauseated me became a source of physical and spiritual consolation for me. After that I did not wait long before I left the world.[10]

For Francis, "leaving the world" seems to have meant choosing to live exclusively as Christ's disciple.

Occasionally Francis stopped to pray at the dilapidated chapel of San Damiano, which was located about a half mile outside of Assisi. One day early in 1206, as he knelt in prayer before the crucifix over the altar, the image of Christ moved its lips and spoke to him. "Francis," the Lord said, "go repair my house, which you see is falling completely to ruin."[11] Stunned to the core, Francis had two responses. His whole being flooded with love for Christ crucified, which from that day oriented his entire life. His biographer speculated that Christ implanted his wounds deep in Francis's heart before he imprinted them on his body.[12] Then taking the Lord's words literally, he jumped up, ready to obey the Lord's command— as he understood it—to repair the ramshackle building.

The San Damiano reconstruction project would need money. Francis knew exactly how to get it. He gathered up expensive bolts of cloth from his father's shop and took them on horseback to Foligno. He quickly sold them and the horse as well. He returned on foot to San Damiano, where he offered the money to the elderly priest who took care of the chapel. The priest wisely refused the donation because he feared reprisals from Francis's father, whose reputation for fury was well deserved.

Rage got the better of Pietro di Bernardone when he discovered what his son had done. He dragged Francis home, beat him, and locked him in a cellar. He hoped his severe treatment would win both the return of his money and the return of his son to his senses. While Pietro was traveling on business, Francis's mother, Pica, who doted on him, released him. When Pietro returned, he rounded up Francis and hauled him before the local bishop's court. At a public hearing in the square outside his palace, Bishop Guido, a friend and adviser of Francis, told him to give the money back. "Gladly, my Lord," said Francis, "and I will do even more."[13]

He went into the building, removed his clothes, reappeared holding them, and stood naked before the crowd. He threw everything on the ground and said, "From now on, I can freely say 'our Father who art in heaven,' not 'father Pietro di Bernardone.' I give him back not only the money, but all the clothes that he has given me. I will now go naked before the Lord."[14] Defeated and fuming, Pietro slipped away. Thus Francis renounced his inheritance, broke his family ties, and chose to depend on God alone.

Francis went to Gubbio, where a friend gave him some clothing. Happily he dressed as a hermit, wearing a simple tunic, belt, and sandals and carrying a staff. He spent several months caring for lepers at Gubbio. Then in summer 1206 he retuned home to Assisi. For the next year and a half, until February, 2008, Francis repaired the churches of San Damiano, San Pietro, and Santa Maria degli Angeli, also called Portiuncula. He consolidated his spiritual growth by continuing to pray and serve the poor.

The climax of Francis's conversion occurred in February 1208. He attended Mass at the Portiuncula on February 24, the feast of St. Matthias. The words of the Gospel stabbed Francis with conviction:

> And as you go, proclaim that the kingdom of Heaven is close at hand. Cure the sick, raise the dead, cleanse those suffering from virulent skin-diseases, drive out devils. You received without charge, give without charge. Provide yourselves with no gold or silver, not even with coppers for your purses, with no haversack for the journey or spare tunic or footwear or a staff, for the laborer deserves his keep. (Matthew 10:7–13)

MERCY UNBOUNDED
BLESSED FRANCIS XAVIER SEELOS (1819–1867)

Many people came to conversion when they experienced God's unlimited mercy through the ministry of Fr. Francis Seelos, a Redemptorist priest who was famous as a compassionate confessor.

Oh, if only all the sinners of the whole wide world were present here! Yes, even the greatest, the most hardened, even those close to despair. I would call out to them. 'The Lord God is merciful and gracious, patient and of much compassion' (Exodus 34:6). I would show them why the Apostles call God the Father of Mercy, the God of all consolation. I would tell them that the prophet in the Old Testament even said that the earth is full of the mercy of God and that mercy is above all his works.

Oh, how can I make this clear to you? First, that God is filled with pity and invites us lovingly to come to him? That God waits for the conversion of the whole world with patience? And thirdly, that God receives the repentant sinner with all love.

O, Mary, Mother of Mercy! You understood the mercy of God when you cried out in the Magnificat: 'His mercy is from generation to generation.' Obtain for all sinners a childlike confidence in the mercy of God.

O, you sinners who have not the courage to confess your sins because they are so numerous or so grievous or so shameful! Oh, come without fear or trembling! I promise to receive you with all mildness. If I do not keep my word, I here publicly give you permission to throw it up to me in the confessional and to charge me with lying.

—FRANCIS XAVIER SEELOS. "Sermons," Redemptorist Archives, Baltimore Province, III, 21; 228, 230.

Francis took these words as the Lord's charge for his life. "This is what I want," he said. "This is what I seek, this is what I long to do with all my heart."[15] He took the Lord's direction literally. He shed his shoes, belt, and staff and made himself a rough tunic that resembled a cross and tied it with a simple cord. Then he began his life's work, preaching a simple version of the gospel by word and example to the people of Assisi and the surrounding towns.

BEYOND OURSELVES

Thanks solely to this encounter—or renewed encounter—with God's love, which blossoms into an enriching friendship, we are liberated from our narrowness and self-absorption. We become fully human when we become more than human, when we let God bring us beyond ourselves in order to attain the fullest truth of our being. Here we find the source and inspiration of all our efforts at evangelization. For if we have received the love which restores meaning to our lives, how can we fail to share that love with others?

—POPE FRANCIS, *The Joy of the Gospel*, 8

The conversion Francis experienced between 1200 and 1208 had oriented him for a life of faith in, and obedience to, Christ crucified. Soon he was joined by a band of brothers, whom he formed into a religious community that embraced his vision and ideals. Francis had finally become a knight—not in the service of a secular king, but in the service of the Lord. Married to Lady Poverty and surrounded by his friars, whom he called the knights of his round table, he launched a movement that renewed Christianity in the Middle Ages and continues to touch hearts in the twenty-first century.

Think, Pray, and Act

Reflect on your relationship to the Lord to assess how well you have responded to the opportunities he has given you to live more fully for him.

Think

🏃 In the process of my conversion, what changes have I made that have drawn me closer to God? What, if any, opportunities have I failed to take for growth or change?

Pray

🏃 Take half an hour to pray, asking the Holy Spirit to identify one or two areas in which you must make some change to advance your ongoing conversion.

Act

🏃 From your reflection, choose one step that you can take to continue your ongoing conversion. Figure out what you must do to accomplish or implement it.

May you seize every opportunity to give yourself more fully to God. And may you respond daily to occasions of grace that will make you more and more like Christ.

Four CALLING

I shall instruct you and teach you the way to go;
I shall not take my eyes off you.
—*Psalm 32:8*

Today the Lord continues to call others to follow him. We should not wait to be perfect . . . , but open our hearts to the voice of the Lord. To listen to that voice, to discern our personal mission in the Church and the world, and at last to live it in the today that God gives us.
—POPE FRANCIS, Message for World Day of Vocations, December 3, 2017

You have heard the voice of God.

You may not be aware of it, but God is speaking to you. He is calling you to come to him. He yearns for you and wants to give you the gift of himself. He whispers his desire for you in your heart, and you may sense his voice as a deep-seated, unfulfilled longing. He calls you to respond by giving yourself to him. Because he loves you, he wants you to offer yourself freely, so he does not command or force you. Rather he invites you, speaking to you softly through family, friends, choices, failures, circumstances, desires, and many other initiatives of grace. He speaks especially through your desires because they reflect his desire for you.

Sometimes he calls a person to a specific service, perhaps as a priest, a minister, a religious, or a missionary. But he calls most of us to serve in worldly enterprises where we can make him present in family, jobs, service, politics, and play. "Every Christian ought to grow in the ability to 'read within' his or her life," said Pope Francis, "and to understand where and to what he or she is being called by the Lord, in order to carry on his mission."[1] And he may be asking you to do something for him, possibly to devote more time to prayer and helping others.

God called St. Katharine Drexel to a special work, the founding of a religious community that would serve Native Americans and African Americans. As you read about the ways that God spoke to her, listen carefully. You may hear him say something to you.

To many twenty-first-century minds that are preoccupied with self and stuff, St. Katharine Drexel is an enigma. An heiress to a huge fortune who could have had anything she desired and done anything she wanted, she preferred poverty to wealth, simplicity to extravagance, praying to partying, and service to self-importance. Once a lovely debutante, a prize for wealthy suitors, an attractive socialite who could have dominated the Philadelphia scene, she instead spent her life and her millions serving the most marginalized people in America. In a real sense Katharine got everything she desired and did everything she wanted, for she had her heart set on loving God, and he called her to give her all for African Americans and Native Americans (or "Indians," which was the name commonly used at the time).

I regard Katharine Drexel as an icon of the appropriate human response to God's call. My reflection on her spiritual pathway has opened me to listen more attentively for the diverse ways God is speaking to me. Widowed after fifty-one years of happy marriage with Mary Lou and the proud father of a large family with sixteen grandkids, I don't expect him to reorient my primary vocation. But I suspect God has some things to say to me as a father and as his disciple, and I want to be sure to pick up his signals. It helps me to watch St. Katharine struggling to figure out what God wanted of her, because I also struggle with discerning where he is leading me. And just as she matched her will to his by considering her desires, circumstances, relationships, and opportunities, I want to do the same.

CALLED TO DAILY SERVICE
SAINT JOHN HENRY NEWMAN (1801–1890)

The great convert and cardinal taught that we meet Christ by faithfully performing the duties of our vocation, no matter how ordinary.

When persons are convinced life is short . . . and that eternity is the only subject that really can claim or can fill our thoughts, then they are apt to undervalue this life altogether, and to forget its real importance. They are apt to wish to spend the time of their sojourning here in a positive separation from active and social duties: yet it should be recollected that the employments of this world, though not themselves heavenly, are after all the way to heaven . . . but it is difficult to realize this. It is difficult to realize both truths at once, and to connect both truths together. . . . In various ways does the thought of the next world lead men to neglect their duty in this; and whenever it does so we may be sure that there is something wrong and unchristian, not in their thinking of the next world, but in their manner of thinking of it. . . .

The Christian will feel that the true contemplation of his Savior lies in his worldly business; that as Christ is seen in the poor, and in the persecuted, . . . so is he seen in the employments he puts upon his chosen . . . ; that in attending to his own calling he will be meeting Christ; that if he neglect it, he will not on that account enjoy his presence at all the more, but that while performing it, he will see Christ revealed to his soul amid the ordinary actions of the day, as by a sort of sacrament.

—JOHN HENRY NEWMAN, "Doing Glory to God in Pursuits of the World," in Charles Davis, ed., *English Spiritual Writers* (New York: Sheed & Ward, 1961), 145.

God first called Katharine through her family. During her childhood, Francis A. Drexel, her father, amassed great wealth in his banking business. We might fairly expect the Drexels to match the stereotype of the *nouveaux riche*—showy, materialistic, self-absorbed, elitist, and arrogant. But they did not fit this pattern—far from it. Kate, as she was called, had been born into a family strongly shaped by Christian values that affluence did not distort or erode.

Amassing millions did not divert Francis Drexel from his sense of Christian purpose. He looked at life through the lens of an eternal perspective. In 1858, for example, upon the loss of his first wife, who died five weeks after Kate's birth, he wrote to a friend about his faith: "If I know myself I am resigned to the dispensation of the Almighty. His will in all things be done for he ordereth all things wisely and well. . . . I have every assurance that my beloved one has gone to her heavenly home."[2] Francis cultivated his faith with a regimen of spiritual disciplines, including a half hour of private prayer each day when he returned home from the office.

In 1860 Francis married Emma Bouvier, who cared tenderly for Kate and her sister Elizabeth, and later her sister Louise, who was born to Francis and Emma in 1863. When the girls were old enough, Emma often took them to weekday Mass. There a love for Christ in the Eucharist infected young Kate with a healthy contagion that later became a hallmark of her spirituality. Emma also designated a special room in the Drexel home for personal prayer. Francis and Emma gathered there nightly with their daughters to close the day with the Rosary. "Praying was like breathing," recalled Katharine many years later,

> there was no compulsion, no obligation. it was natural to pray. . . . We were usually in bed by eight o'clock, when we were children. Then in our little night-dresses we would go

to the top of the stairs and call down, "Mama! Papa!" Then Papa . . . would leave his organ or his paper and Mama her writing, and both at the call of the children would come up and kneel for night prayers in the little oratory.[3]

Francis and Emma regarded themselves as stewards of the wealth God had bestowed on them, and they shared generously with the poor. On several days each week Emma welcomed needy people at her door, giving them food, clothing, and money. She trained Kate and her sisters for Christian service by having them help with this distribution. And she expected them to contribute their own money to the work. Emma called this her "Dorcas" ministry, named for the disciple described in the Acts of the Apostles as "never tired of doing good or giving to those in need."[4] Like this namesake, Emma was a tireless giver. Every year she distributed to the poor as much as twenty thousand dollars, plus rent for one hundred fifty families, which in the early years of the twentieth century was a very large sum of money.[5]

As a teenager Katharine kept notebooks that show how the Drexel family spirituality had captivated her. Like her father, already in her youth she saw eternity gleaming through earthly things. Many teens love God, but few are able to share young Katharine's precocious gift for expressing spiritual realities. "The mountains before us," she once wrote while traveling, "Madison, Jefferson, Adams, Clay, Mt. W., and other surrounding peaks, can never be made soft and beautiful, . . . by any sunset. They can never melt into the heavens like beautiful Jacob's ladders as some mountains do; but they remind one, in their might, bald grandeur, firmness, and solidity of eternity—the time that was, the time that will be."[6]

At fifteen Kate prayed forty-five minutes a day and adopted little practices of self-denial to overcome what she regarded as pride and vanity. Fr. James O'Connor, a local pastor and family friend, took an interest in Kate and gently guided her Christian growth. He became her spiritual director, a role he performed until his death in 1890. In 1876 when O'Connor left Pennsylvania to become the bishop of Omaha, Nebraska, he instructed Kate to listen attentively for God's call. "My spiritual father has told me," she wrote, "that my predominant passion is scrupulosity. His parting advice to me was always to pray fervently to God each day that He might aid me to know my vocation in life. He dwelt at length on the importance of this prayer. I am to write him in any difficulty whatsoever."[7] Among Katharine's daily prayers was the *Veni Sancte Spiritus*, the powerful invocation of the Holy Spirit that clarified the calling of many other saints.

Cancer struck Emma Drexel late in 1879, and for three years Katharine hovered at her bedside. She wept in anguish over her mother's extreme suffering. Watching her mother slip away and reflecting on her years of heroic generosity, Katharine began to entertain an irrepressible notion that she should enter the religious life.

Emma died in January 1883. Five months later, Katharine sent Bishop O'Connor a list of pros and cons of joining a religious community, hoping he would side with the pros. O'Connor was not impressed. He told her that her positives—that included self-sacrifice, perfect love of God, overcoming the flesh, and a high reward in heaven—were impersonal, abstract, and general. But her negatives raised warning flags, especially her avowed distaste for community life and abhorrence of obedience to an unworthy superior.[8] In her subsequent letters Katharine continued to express impatience about determining the course of her life. O'Connor restrained her with advice to "think, pray, wait."[9]

Katharine's father contracted pleurisy in February 1885, and although he recovered temporarily, he died unexpectedly while she was attending him. Her grief was unimaginable, losing her beloved father so soon after her mother's death. The events that followed complicated Katharine's future by prolonging the uncertainty of her life's direction.

Francis Drexel left his daughters equal shares of the annual income from fourteen million dollars held for them in trust. Like their parents, the sisters immediately looked for opportunities to use their wealth in support of the poor. They did not have to wait long. Shortly after Mr. Drexel's death, Fr. Joseph Stephan, director of the Bureau of Catholic Indian Missions, visited Katharine and appealed for help in building and staffing schools for Indian children. Without hesitation she contributed to the construction of centers in Montana and New Mexico, thus beginning a lifelong friendship with Fr. Stephan and ministry to Native Americans. A year later she started her service to African Americans by purchasing a building in Philadelphia to be used by the Sisters of Notre Dame as a "school for the colored."

The opportunity to use her inheritance to aid the poor created a new tension for Katherine. Her heart aspired to the contemplative life of a cloistered nun, but it also ached to help Native Americans and African Americans, whom she recognized as the most neglected people in the country. Trips to Europe and the western United States tugged her in the direction of an active life in the world. On a visit to the Vatican in 1886 she asked Pope Leo XIII to send priests as missionaries to Native Americans. The pope stabbed her with a response she never forgot: "Why not, my child, yourself become a missionary?"[10] In 1886 and 1887 Katharine accompanied Fr. Stephan on tours of the missions she had funded in the West from South Dakota to Washington. Personal contact with her poor beneficiaries heightened her love for them, but at the same time her desire for a life of quiet prayer grew even more.

DISCERNING CHRIST'S EXPECTATIONS

You need to see the entirety of your life as a mission. Try to do so by listening to God in prayer and recognizing the signs that he gives you. Always ask the Spirit what Jesus expects from you at every moment of your life and in every decision you must make, so as to discern its place in the mission you have received. Allow the Spirit to forge in you the personal mystery that can reflect Jesus Christ in today's world.

—POPE FRANCIS, *Rejoice and Be Glad,* 23

Katharine poured out her frustration in a series of exchanges with Bishop O'Connor. She wondered why she could not establish a bureau that would distribute her money to the causes of Indians and blacks. Because, the bishop replied, she had the charism for serving these "most abandoned and forlorn" peoples, and a board would not do it with as much fervor and care as she would. But in the end, Katharine's restless hunger for the religious life won out. On November 26, 1888, her twenty-eighth birthday, she informed the bishop that she had decided to become a nun. "Do not, Reverend Father," she wrote,

> I beseech you, say "What is to become of your work?" What is to become of it when I shall give it all to Our Lord? . . . Are you afraid to give me to Jesus Christ? God knows how unworthy I am, and yet can He not supply my unworthiness *if* only He gives me a vocation to the religious life? Then joyfully I run to Him. I am afraid to receive your answer to this note.[11]

Katharine did not need to fear, for the bishop responded immediately approving of her decision and recommending religious communities for her consideration. She determined to find a community that served Indian and black people and that practiced frequent reception of the Eucharist, which was not the norm at the time. Then the bishop startled her in February 1889 with a new suggestion. He strongly recommended that she found her own religious order dedicated to care for the marginalized people she had come to love.

Katharine resisted with a series of objections: she desired the contemplative life and daily Communion; she did not have the virtue or gift to start a new order; an established order could do the work without the red tape required to start a new one; the combined effort of many orders working together would do a better job. O'Connor assured Katharine that founding a new order was God's will for her. He easily dismissed her concerns as "scruples." Her rule could require daily Communion. God would supply gifts that would compensate for her weaknesses. New orders always rose up to meet new needs. And although existing orders could help in the work, the ministry required the exclusive attention of one dedicated community.[12]

Apparently, Katharine was more open to the idea than her initial response to the bishop had indicated. Prayer melted any residual resistance, and a month later she agreed to found her own religious order. "The Feast of St. Joseph," she wrote, "brought me the grace to give the remainder of my life to the Indians and colored, to enter fully and entirely into your views . . . as to what is best for the salvation of the souls of these people."[13]

Katharine's long quest for her vocation had reached its goal.

After two years of preparation and training, on February 12, 1891, she made her profession and founded the Sisters of the Blessed Sacrament. To vows of poverty, chastity, and obedience, she added a fourth: to be the mother and servant of Native Americans and African Americans and not to undertake any work that would lead to neglecting or abandoning them.

For the next four decades Mother Katharine spent herself in active service tempered with prayer. She formed her sisters and trained them for missionary work. By 1904, 104 women had joined her community. Katharine traversed the country many times, selecting sites for missions and visiting established centers. She and her sisters founded 145 missions and twelve schools for Native Americans and fifty schools for African Americans. In 1915 Katharine proudly established Xavier University in New Orleans, the first Catholic college for black youth in the United States. Throughout her life she contributed about twenty million dollars for these causes.

St. Katharine Drexel heard God's call in the circumstances of her life. He spoke to her through a father who viewed everything from the perspective of eternity and devoted himself and his wealth to pursuing it. Katherine heard God's voice in her mother, who taught her to pray and trained her in generous service to the poor. She sensed his calling her in her compassion for Native Americans and African Americans. God guided her through the spiritual director, who helped her map the course of her life. He appealed to her in the words of a pope, who suggested that she become a missionary. Most of all, Katharine heard God's call in her irrepressible desire to give herself to him in prayer.

And after Katharine had spent forty years serving God on his terms, he granted her youthful wish for a life dedicated simply to him. In 1935 a serious heart attack slowed her down, and two years later she retired. Then she got her heart's desire and enjoyed eighteen years of quiet contemplation before her death in 1955 at the age of ninety-seven. As Scripture promises, "Take delight in the Lord, and he will give you the desires of your heart" (Psalm 37:4, RSV).

Think

- In what ways has God called me and guided me through my life? Through Scripture? Life circumstances? Family members or friends? Advisers? The pope? (just kidding, but maybe not).

- When God sought to redirect me, how sensitive was I to his leadings?

Pray

Set aside half an hour of quiet prayer and reflect on the following questions.

- What do I think God may be saying to me now?

- Is he asking me to make any change in the way I am conducting my life? What does he seem to want me to do?

Act

- What one action might I take to respond to God's call now?

May you hear God's call and discern his will for your life in your daily circumstances. May you listen carefully for his direction in the words of your relatives, your friends, your pastor and fellow parishioners, your neighbors, your colleagues, and in your casual encounters.

𝓕𝓲𝓿𝓮 PRAYER AND STUDY
DOROTHY DAY (1897–1980)

Always be joyful; pray constantly; and for all things give thanks;
this is the will of God for you in Christ Jesus.
—*1 Thessalonians 5:16–18*

The saints are distinguished by a spirit of prayer and a need
for communion with God. They find an exclusive concern
with this world to be narrow and stifling, and, amid their
own concerns and commitments, they long for God, losing
themselves in praise and contemplation of the Lord.
—POPE FRANCIS, *Rejoice and Be Glad,* 147

Just because I *feel* that everything is useless and going to
pieces and badly done and futile, it is not really that way at all.
Everything is all right. It is in the hands of God. Let us abandon
everything to Divine Providence.
—DOROTHY DAY

*At the beginning of his public ministry Jesus announced the coming
of the kingdom of God. He was declaring that in his person, God was
already overthrowing the forces of evil and setting things right in the
world. For proof that God was on the move, Jesus went about healing
the sick and delivering people from the influence of evil spirits. He
invited men and women to collaborate with him in building God's
kingdom and taught them a new way of living. His followers would
be a light to the world. They would manifest the presence of the*

kingdom by living according to his high standard. They would set their hearts on serving God, depend on God for everything, forgive all offenders, work for peace, and accept persecution. They would also give generously, live chastely, love their enemies, and respond to evil with good. Then finally by his death and resurrection, Jesus established the kingdom, launching God's great project of reclaiming us and the earth.

All Christians share in Christ's ministry of restoring all people and things that evil has corrupted. We each have our own part to play in God's story told in the gospels. He taps each of us for a particular role in his saving work and gives us the gifts we need to accomplish it. In order to ensure that we perform well, he has given us the Bible as a guide, and he directs us personally in our prayer.

So prayer and Scripture study are the primary ways that we live out our Christian calling. In both activities we are communicating with God. In both we come into his presence and carry on conversations with him. In prayer we express our love for him, thank him, and ask him for our needs, and he speaks to us in our heart and thoughts. When we study his word in Scripture, we also hear his voice and learn what he wants of us and for us.

Prayer and study occupy a big place in the heart of every saint. So I could have shown how any saint employed these means of Christian growth. But I chose Dorothy Day, who is a "Servant of God" on her way to canonization, for two reasons. First, I wanted to write about her because for five decades she spent herself collaborating with Christ to combat the evils of poverty and injustice with kindness and care. And prayer and Scripture study carried her through hardships that confronted her every day. Second, I chose her because I think we as busy people can relate easily to the way she fit prayer and study into her very hectic days as a single parent, caregiver, social activist, community organizer, and writer.

One cold morning Dorothy Day gently chastised a young volunteer at a Catholic Worker house. She told Stanley Vishnewski that by missing daily Mass he was "hurting the work." The work she had in mind was the work of the church in continuing Christ's ministry of mercy and justice.

After Dorothy became a Catholic she discovered the doctrine of the Mystical Body of Christ, and she incarnated it. The truths about the Mystical Body delighted her: that Christ prayed in her and millions of others when she joined his worship at Mass and in the Liturgy of the Hours; that in the invisible, heavenly sector of the Mystical Body she had communion with thousands of saints; that the Lord himself continued his ministry through her daily service to the poor and marginalized; and that he strengthened her when she grew so tired that she felt she might not be able to go on. Animated by Christ's presence, Dorothy embodied corporal and spiritual works of mercy. She fed the hungry, housed the homeless, counseled the doubtful, and bore all wrongs patiently— even when she felt like striking back at her critics. Pope Francis may have had saints like Dorothy in mind when he said, "Those who really wish to give glory to God by their lives, who truly long to grow in holiness, are called to be single-minded and tenacious in their practice of the works of mercy."[1]

Dorothy wanted her colleagues to embrace the realities of the Mystical Body as well. "We cannot live alone," she said. "We cannot go to heaven alone. Otherwise . . . God will say to us, 'Where are the others?'"[2] That's why she told young Vishnewski that his missing daily Mass diminished the effectiveness of the ministry.

At her instigation and that of Peter Maurin, her mentor, the Catholic Worker movement evolved as a significant expression of the Mystical Body of Christ. And although the Lord directed and empowered Dorothy and her associates, his presence did not make the work easy. Caring for the destitute remained hard and thankless. Prayer and study of Scripture had led Dorothy to accept the call to this ministry. And it was prayer and Scripture that sustained her in the work.

Dorothy Day's immersion in prayer and Scripture began in her childhood and extended throughout her life. She first encountered God when she was seven, while playing with her sister Della. In 1904 the Day family had moved from Brooklyn Heights, New York, Dorothy's birthplace, to Berkeley, California. In the attic of the rented home where they lived, Dorothy found a Bible. Pretending to be a school teacher, she began to read aloud from it. Later, she did not recall the text she had opened to, but she remembered that she had sensed something stirring within her as she read. She reckoned that Someone had come near to her, and the experience left her awestruck. "I knew almost immediately that I was discovering God," she wrote,

> I knew that I had just really discovered Him because it excited me tremendously. It was as though life were fuller, richer, more exciting in every way. Here was someone that I had never really known about before and yet felt to be One whom I would never forget, that I would never get away from. . . . I had made a great discovery. . . . It was that Sunday afternoon up in that dim attic and the rich, deep feeling of having a book, which would be with me through life, that stands out in my mind now.[3]

Reading Scripture prayerfully, as she had done unintentionally during a game of "let's pretend," became Dorothy's lifelong habit.

The Day family fled California when the San Francisco earthquake of April 1906 destroyed their home and impoverished them. They moved to a poor neighborhood in South Chicago. While there eight-year-old Dorothy had some early experiences of prayer that she never forgot. One morning she barged in on her neighbor, Mrs. Barrett, and found her kneeling in prayer. "All through my life what she was doing remained with me. And though I became oppressed with the problem of poverty and injustice . . . life was shot through with glory. Mrs. Barrett in her sordid little tenement flat finished her breakfast dishes at ten o'clock in the morning and got down on her knees and prayed to God."[4] Insertion of personal prayer in the flow of daily activities would also become one of Dorothy's habitual practices.

At the age of ten, Dorothy acquired her enduring appreciation for liturgical prayer. She attended the liturgy every Sunday at an Episcopal church where two of her brothers sang in the choir. She recalled in *The Long Loneliness*, her autobiography, that she loved the psalms and canticles of *The Book of Common Prayer* and memorized many of them.

> I had never heard anything so beautiful as the *Benedicite* and the *Te Deum*. . . . The song thrilled in my heart, and though I was only ten years old, through these Psalms and canticles I called on all creation to join with me in blessing the Lord. I thanked him for creating me, saving me from all evils, and filling me with all good things.[5]

As Dorothy matured, and especially after she converted to Catholicism, liturgical prayer permeated her thought, her service to the poor, her relationships with family and friends—in short, all her days.

❧

From her youth Dorothy Day read books voraciously. At fifteen, in addition to the New Testament, she devoured the novels of Dickens, Jack London's essays on the class struggle, and Upton Sinclair's *The Jungle*. The latter especially intrigued her because it described Chicago's poverty, which she had experienced firsthand. She was also reading the *Day Book,* a paper for which her older brother Donald had signed on as a writer. The paper focused on Chicago's labor issues. In its pages Dorothy became acquainted with the idealism of contributing poet Carl Sandburg, socialist Eugene V. Debs, and the International Workers of the World (IWW).[6]

At the same time Dorothy was an avid "reader" of the conditions of Chicago's poor. With her baby brother John and sister Della in tow, she frequently walked for miles through the city's bleak streets, observing with compassion the squalor and suffering of her neighbors. Her reading and her walks persuaded young Dorothy that she should devote herself to relieving the suffering of the poor. "Though my only experience of the destitute was in books," she wrote,

> the very fact that *The Jungle* was about Chicago where I lived, whose streets I walked, made me feel that from then on my life was to be linked to theirs, their interests were to be mine; I had received a call, a vocation, a direction to my life.[7]

In retrospect, Dorothy could look back after long years of hard work and interpret these experiences as launching her career of service to the poor. But as a teenager she had just begun to form her views. Reading the New Testament and *The Imitation of Christ* in her last years of high school led her to conclude that most Christians ignored the scriptural counsels about caring for the poor. Rarely did she see anyone sharing food, clothing, or money.[8]

In 1914 Dorothy left home to attend the University of Illinois on a three-hundred-dollar scholarship. During her two years at school she embraced radical views. She decided that she could no longer tolerate the way Christians neglected the poor. She joined the Socialist Party, and while she rarely attended meetings, she identified with its program. "Workers of the world unite!" made more sense to her than "Servants, be subject to your masters with all fear" (see Ephesians 6:5). The apparent passivity of the New Testament to injustice persuaded Dorothy to break her ties with organized religion and temporarily to stop reading the Bible. But she maintained her faith in God, nourishing it with the novels of Dostoevsky and Tolstoy.[9]

Dorothy moved to New York when her family relocated there in the summer of 1916. Recognizing her writing gift, she was determined to use it as a journalist to advance the cause of the poor. For the next two years she worked for a series of activist papers. She befriended nonreligious radicals and made no pretense of being Christian. Later, however, she admitted that even then she had believed in the biblically based works of mercy.[10]

Late in 1917 Dorothy traveled with a friend to Washington, DC, to participate in a suffragist demonstration at the White House. As she had expected, she was arrested and detained under miserable conditions at the Occoquan workhouse. Oppressed by cold, darkness, and hunger and fatigued by lack of sleep, she turned to the Bible for comfort. "I read it," she said, "with the sense of coming back to something of my childhood that I had lost. My heart swelled with joy and thankfulness for the Psalms. The man who sang these songs knew sorrow and expected joy."[11] Yet she was conflicted about turning to God, feeling that she wanted to rise above her miseries by her own strength. "I tried to persuade myself that I was reading for literary enjoyment. But the words kept echoing in my heart. I prayed and did not know that I prayed."[12]

In the winter of 1917–1918, Dorothy wrote for several radical journals. She spent her evenings with writers and artists in Greenwich Village, where conversations swirled around the recent Bolshevik takeover in Russia. At one of these gatherings her friend Eugene O'Neill, the playwright, touched her heart by reciting "The Hound of Heaven," Francis Thompson's poem about God's relentless pursuit. Dorothy realized then that she could run, cover her tracks, but never hide.[13] Often after these all-night sessions, she attended early Mass at a nearby church, sitting in the back and taking comfort in the spirit of worship.

Over the next several years, a confusion of relationships plunged Dorothy into turmoil. In November 1918 she began living with another journalist, but the affair ended abruptly in September 1919. He left Dorothy after she aborted his baby in an attempt to preserve the relationship. In 1920 she married a literary agent and went to Europe with him, but they soon realized their incompatibility and separated. When Dorothy came back to the United States in 1921, she relocated to Chicago and divorced him.[14] She did not discuss the deterioration of these relationships or the abortion in her autobiography but left to our imagination their terrible emotional impact. I refrain from judging Dorothy's behavior in these matters and I urge others to do the same. She was loving the poor and looking for love herself, and Christ remained with her despite her wrongdoing.

In the winter of 1921, Dorothy renewed her relationship with God through prayer and Scripture and discovered within herself an openness to the Catholic Church. At the time she shared a room with a young woman named Blanche, who worked as a hatmaker from her home. That Blanche and her sister, both devout Catholics, accepted without judgment her radicalism and bohemian lifestyle touched Dorothy. And their example drew her to prayer. "I saw them pray, and the public prayer in the church and Blanche's kneeling down by the table on which was spread out her hats and trimmings did something to me which I could not forget. As with the sight of Mrs. Barrett kneeling beside her bed, this posture, this gesture, convinced me that worship, adoration, thanksgiving, supplication—these were the noblest acts of which men were capable in this life."[15]

Around this time, Dorothy read the novels of French Catholic author J. K. Huysmans, whose descriptions of Catholic life persuaded her that she could be at home in the church without becoming a Catholic. She also read Pascal's *Pensées*, a philosophical reflection on faith and the human condition, and reread Dostoevsky. Both drew her back to the New Testament, which she said she turned to with love.[16] She spent the winter of 1923 in New Orleans, writing sensational articles for a newspaper during the day and worshipping at Benediction in the evening. The news that a publisher had purchased her novel, *The Eleventh Virgin*, for five thousand dollars brought her back to New York. She used the money to purchase a beach house on Staten Island, where she lived pleasantly for several years.

SCRIPTURE—A MUST-READ
Saint John Chrysostom (347–407)

St. John Chrysostom says that laypeople must read Scripture regularly because Bible study strengthens them to counter the temptations that they face in the world each day.

I am always encouraging you to pay attention not only to what is said here in church, but also, when you are at home, to continue constantly in the practice of reading the divine Scriptures. . . . For let not anyone say to me those silly, contemptible words, . . . "Reading the Bible isn't my thing. That's for those . . . who have a way of life without interruptions."

What are you saying, man? It's not your business to pay attention to the Bible because you are distracted by thousands of concerns? Then Bible reading belongs more to you than to the monks! For they do not make as much use of the help of the divine Scriptures as those who always have a great many things to do. . . . But you are always standing in the line of battle and are constantly being hit, so you need more medicine. For not only does your spouse irritate you, but your son annoys you, . . . an enemy schemes against you, a friend envies you, a neighbor insults you, a colleague trips you up. Often a lawsuit impends, poverty distresses, loss of possessions brings sorrow. . . . Numerous powerful inducements to anger and anxiety, to discouragement and grief, to vanity and loss of sense surround us on every side. . . . And so we constantly need the whole range of equipment supplied by Scripture. . . .

Since many things of this kind besiege our soul, we need the divine medicines, so that we might treat the wounds we already have, and so that we might check beforehand the wounds that are not yet, but are going to be, from afar extinguishing the missiles of the devil and repelling them through the constant reading of the divine Scriptures. For it is not possible, not possible for anyone to be saved who does not constantly have the benefit of spiritual reading.

—John Chrysostom, Sermon on Lazarus, 3, trans. Kevin Perrotta. Used by translator's permission.

Early in 1924, Dorothy contracted a common-law marriage with Forster Batterham, an English biologist and an anarchist. He was intolerant of all religion, but Dorothy says that her life with him brought her natural happiness and drew her closer to God.[17] Forster's appreciation for every living thing awakened in Dorothy a fresh love for creation and the Creator. While Forster worked in the city during the week, she enjoyed friendship with her neighbors and the leisure to read Dickens, Tolstoy, Doetoevsky, and especially the New Testament and *The Imitation of Christ.* She remembered the beach years with Forster as a poignant time of peace and happiness. "I was happy," she wrote, "but my very happiness made me know that there was a greater happiness to be obtained from life than any I had ever known. I began to think, to weigh things, and it was at this time that I began consciously to pray more."[18]

In the summer of 1925, Dorothy became pregnant and was filled with bittersweet excitement. The thought that she was co-creating a child with God thrilled her. But she realized with a profound sadness that the child's birth would end her relationship with Forster. For in order to spare her baby the vicissitudes that she had endured, she had determined to have the child baptized Catholic and become Catholic herself. Her early experience with the fellowship and support of radical groups persuaded her that she could not become Catholic without participating fully in the church community. Given Forster's antipathy to all religion, that decision would cause him the great pain of having to leave her.

Tamar Teresa was born on March 4, 1926, and Dorothy was nearly ecstatic with joy. But the imminence of breaking off with the man she deeply loved tainted her exuberance. Dorothy had Tamar baptized in July, but in order to delay the sorrow of ending her marriage, she postponed becoming Catholic. Finally, in December 1927, she severed her relationship with Forster and was received into the church. She recalled that she felt no particular consolation when she first received the sacraments because she wondered whether she had done the right thing. Not only was she abandoning her husband, but she was also abandoning her life in the radical movement. She was crossing over to the other side, joining a church that identified with capitalism, which she still repudiated.[19]

"I loved the Church for Christ made visible," she wrote, "not for itself, because it was so often a scandal to me. [Catholic theologian] Romano Guardini said the Church is the Cross on which Christ was crucified; one could not separate Christ from his Cross, and one must live in a state of permanent dissatisfaction with the Church."[20] This observation summed up Dorothy's relationship to the church. She was both orthodox and obedient, believing all that the church taught and willing to stop whatever she was doing if a bishop told her to do so. But she steadfastly critiqued the church's behaviors that contradicted Christ's teaching and its own social doctrine.

When the Great Depression was reaching full force in the early 1930s, Dorothy observed that no Catholic leadership seemed to emerge in groups that were prepared to help the unemployed. But Dorothy herself would soon begin to play a significant leadership role in the Catholic Church. In 1932 she attended a hunger march in Washington, DC, as a reporter for the Catholic periodicals *America* and *Commonweal.* The experience persuaded her that she should *do* something about injustice rather than merely write about it. Before she left the capital, she went to the National Shrine of the Immaculate Conception and prayed earnestly that some way would open up for her to use her talents to serve the laboring poor.[21] When she returned to New York she found the answer to her prayer in the person of Peter Maurin.

Peter Maurin (1877–1949) was a French peasant, teacher, and itinerant laborer who had wandered about Canada and the United States. He dedicated himself to spreading the social doctrine of the Catholic Church. Peter snared people into roundtable discussions for "clarification of thought" or just buttonholed individuals for the same purpose. He wanted to establish houses of hospitality that would perform the corporal and spiritual works of mercy. In these centers all comers would find food, shelter, and solace. Peter also wanted to create "agronomic universities," a move back to the land where on small farms scholars would learn to be farmers and farmers would learn to be scholars. He undergirded his program with the philosophy of French personalist thinkers, who held that we share a common humanity in which each person would find his destiny by assuming personal responsibility for needy people.[22]

Armed with these ideas, Peter Maurin wanted to build a new social order within the old, one in which it would be "easy for people to be good."[23] Maurin had handpicked Dorothy to help him because of her impressive skills as a journalist. He wanted her to launch a newspaper that would popularize his views and that would ultimately generate a peaceful revolutionary movement. At first Dorothy rejected the idea of starting a paper with no money, but Peter persuaded her by arguing that the saints raised the capital they needed by prayer.[24] So the first issue of *The Catholic Worker* hit the streets on May 1, 1933. Volunteers sold twenty-five hundred copies for a penny each in Union Square. The paper was an instant success. By the end of the year circulation had reached a hundred thousand.

Dorothy wrote about the conditions of the poor, the labor movement, the tenets of Catholic social teaching, and the planks of Peter Maurin's program. Volunteers streamed in to serve at the House of Hospitality that Peter and Dorothy had opened in Manhattan. And soon similar centers appeared in cities throughout the United States. Thus, Peter and Dorothy launched a peaceful movement that would have a revolutionary effect on the Catholic Church.

For nearly fifty years after the paper first appeared, Dorothy lived what she wrote about. She cooked and served food for the hungry who lined up every day; she gave grooming care to guests; she cleaned up the vomit of the sick and changed soiled bed clothes; she counseled the troubled and comforted the sad and desperate; she showed respect to all and special affection for the mentally ill; she traveled extensively, giving her advice to new houses of hospitality and farms; she supported labor strikes; she opposed all war on the basis of Christ's command to love enemies; she wrote "On Pilgrimage," her regular column in *The Catholic Worker;* she challenged bishops when she thought they were wrong, but she never spoke against them, and she did much more, all the while caring for Tamar and eventually her grandchildren. And she lived and conducted all of her service in the presence of God.

We admire holy people like Dorothy Day, who seem to be able to obey the biblical command to "pray constantly" (1 Thessalonians 5:17). She understood "praying constantly" to mean living in God's presence, which she practiced faithfully throughout her Catholic Worker days. She wrote extensively about her experience of prayer because she wanted all of her associates to dwell in God's presence and rely on him to accomplish their work rather than on their own strength. She never wrote a prescription for continuous prayer, but if she had, it would have included three elements: liturgical prayer, *lectio divina,* and intercession.

Dorothy realized that she could pray continuously if she joined the official prayer of the church. For in the Mass and the Liturgy of the Hours, it is Christ who is praying, and we simply join his uninterrupted worship. "When we pray thus," she wrote, "we pray with Christ, not to Christ. When we pray [the hours] of prime and compline we are using the inspired prayer of the church."[25] Liturgical prayer is the prayer of the Mystical Body of Christ, which flows from Christ, the head, to all of us, his members, a reality which Dorothy saw as having significant social implications. "Living the liturgical day as much as we are able," she wrote,

> beginning with prime, using the missal [at Mass], ending the day with compline and so going through the liturgical year we find that it is now not us, but Christ in us, who is working to combat injustice and oppression."[26]

So the more you and I worship at Mass and pray the liturgical hours, the more we will have Christ working through us in our daily activities and service.

Dorothy saw *lectio divina* as another way to pray continuously. *Lectio divina* is Latin for prayerfully reading and meditating on Scripture and other spiritual books. As we have seen, Dorothy loved to reflect on the New Testament, pray the psalms, and study books such as *The Imitation of Christ*. She always expected the Lord to be present to her when she read Scripture, just as it had happened the first time she opened a Bible as a child. As Christians had done from the earliest days, Dorothy saw Christ's presence in the Bible as equivalent to his presence the Eucharist. She once commented on a passage in *The Imitation of Christ* that described the Lord's real presence in Scripture:

> In that most popular book . . . , they compared scripture to the Holy Eucharist. . . . They speak of food and light as necessary for man to grow. The food was the body and blood of Christ and the light was holy scripture. They were put on an equality which is a very awesome thought. It is

as though if we possessed a Bible in the home, . . . we had a private chapel with the blessed sacrament.[27]

Taking a cue from Dorothy Day, we should expect to experience the Lord's presence when we reflect on Scripture or do spiritual reading.

Dorothy Day was also a constant intercessor. She pestered the Lord with frequent aspirations. "There is nothing too small to pray about," she would say as she called on God with a verse often repeated in the liturgy, "O God come to my assistance, O Lord make haste to help me (see Psalm 70:2)."[28] Those who sought her help had titanic needs, but none were too big for God. "I must write about prayer," she said,

> because it is as necessary to life as breathing. It is food and drink. And I must write about it because we here at the Catholic Worker are surrounded by the lame, the halt and the blind, the utterly destitute, and it is a seemingly hopeless situation.[29]

She kept long lists of people in need and often slipped off to a chapel to pray for them.

Dorothy expected God to say yes to her prayers because she prayed with faith. Once, for example, she excitedly said to her associates, "Rejoice, rejoice! All of you, rejoice. We're all going to heaven because I have asked our Lord every single day of my life that everyone who comes [here] will be saved."[30] She even believed that she could pray about things that happened in the past because God existed outside of time and was not limited by it.[31] Dorothy regularly reported answered prayers in her column "On Pilgrimage," ranging from reconciling opponents at a House of Hospitality to acquiring a large parcel of land for a Catholic Worker farm. So, constant intercession was Dorothy Day's way of praying always, and it is a practice that we can easily imitate.

PRAYER THAT PLEASES GOD

It is true that the primacy belongs to our relationship with God, but we cannot forget that the ultimate criterion on which our lives will be judged is what we have done for others. Prayer is most precious, for it nourishes a daily commitment to love. Our worship becomes pleasing to God when we devote ourselves to living generously, and allow God's gift, granted in prayer, to be shown in our concern for our brothers and sisters.

—POPE FRANCIS, *Rejoice and Be Glad,* 104

Through prayer and Scripture, the Lord accompanied Dorothy Day, guiding her in her ministry to the poor. Occasionally he let her know that he was right there beside her. "You know," she once confided to a friend, "sometimes when I was so discouraged, I'd feel a hand on my shoulder and it would be Jesus' hand."[32] And led and sustained by him, Dorothy Day left a legacy of generous service that anticipated the social justice issues now championed by the official church, including preferential concern for the poor, defense of all human life from conception to natural death, and advocacy for peace.

Many laypeople, priests, and bishops regarded Dorothy as a living saint, but she would have none of it. "Don't call me a saint," she was known to say. "I don't want to be dismissed that easily." But the church ignored her wish. At the request of Cardinal John J. O'Connor in March 2000, Pope John Paul II granted the Archdiocese of New York permission to open her cause, allowing her to be called a "Servant of God." And the bishops of the United States unanimously endorsed her sainthood cause during their 2012 fall general assembly. Dorothy still may not like it very much, but the process for her canonization is underway.

Think, Pray, and Act

Review your approach to prayer and reading of Scripture and spiritual books. Use the following questions to help you learn to practice the presence of God more effectively.

Think

🏃 What is my experience of liturgical prayer? Do I look forward to and participate in Sunday Mass? Do I worship at daily Mass? How often? Do I pray any of the Liturgy of the Hours?

🏃 How often do I read and reflect on Scripture? What type of spiritual books do I read? What other spiritual books have I read recently?

🏃 Do I make time of personal prayer daily? How faithful am I to that time? Have I found a time and place to pray each day without distractions?

🏃 How often do I intercede for the needs I observe in others? Do I keep a list of people and things to pray for? Do I intercede with short aspirations throughout the day?

Pray

🏃 Take half an hour of quiet prayer to reflect on your current efforts to pray and study. Ask the Holy Spirit to show you what you might do to enhance your ability to live in the presence of God.

Act

🏃 Select one thing that you could easily do to improve your prayer or study. Decide to do it faithfully for a predetermined period of time, such as a month. At the end of the time period, look back on how you did. Make any adjustment you might need, and repeat the practice for another period or until it becomes a habit.

May you immerse yourself in God's presence through daily prayer and Scripture study. And may the Lord show you ways and give you the strength to serve poor and marginalized people.

Six COMMUNITY
SAINT ANGELA MERICI (C. 1474–1540)

Each day, with one heart, they regularly went to the Temple but met in their houses for the breaking of bread; . . . they praised God and were looked up to by everyone. Day by day the Lord added to their community those destined to be saved.

—*Acts 2:46–47*

Be on your guard and especially take care to be of one heart and mind, just as we read of the apostles and the other Christians of the early Church. . . . Loving and being united to one another is the only sign that pleases the Lord.

—ST. ANGELA MERICI, *Testament*

Growth in holiness is a journey in community, side by side with others.

—POPE FRANCIS, *Rejoice and Be Glad,* 141.

From the earliest days of his public ministry, Jesus attracted crowds. It wasn't long before a large number of "regulars" followed after him and constituted an informal community. If you had noticed Jesus coming down the dusty road to your town, you would not have seen an itinerant preacher with a few attendants, but a sizeable company of women and men, who accompanied him everywhere. So, from the very outset, Jesus was drawing people into the assembly that he would finally establish as the church, the body of believers that would continue his work of renewing the face of the earth.

The Lord founded the church as a community. And he made unity one of its chief marks, which we traditionally list as one, holy, catholic, and apostolic. As the church increased in numbers, it evolved into a community of communities scattered throughout the world. From the first century to the present, every age has seen the Holy Spirit prompt the formation of communities that responded to the needs of the church and society. Looking back through the ages we can catalog a great diversity of lay and religious communities, beginning at the citywide Jerusalem assembly that celebrated the Eucharist in home groups down to the vast multiplicity of parishes, religious orders, and communal movements of our own day. Even in the fourth century when men like St. Anthony (251–356) and St. Pachomius (c. 292–346) left the world to dwell with God in the solitude of the desert, they gathered others around them. We cannot mention the great saints of the Middle Ages, such as Benedict (c. 480– c. 543), Francis (1181–1226), Clare (1194–1253), Dominic (1170– 1221), and Catherine of Siena (1347–1380), without remembering that they assembled communities that transformed their worlds.

In revolutionary and war-torn sixteenth-century Europe, saints also started experimental and reformed communities for men and women. In France and Italy, St. Ignatius of Loyola (1491–1556) organized the Society of Jesus, a community of men devoted to making disciples through evangelization and education. In Spain, St. Teresa of Avila (1515–1582) founded or reformed seventeen Carmelite communities of women that helped revive contemplative life in that country. In Rome, St. Philip Neri (1515–1595) founded the Oratory, a creative association of priests. He and his brothers generated spontaneous lay communities by regularly gathering people for evenings of prayer and study that often ended with a concert or short pilgrimage. And to the north in Lombardy, St. Angela Merici established an innovative community for women, whose members were committed to a high Christian ideal and to each other, but who lived at home with their families and served as catechists in their local parishes.

To their great disadvantage, many contemporary Catholics and other Christians find it difficult to participate in a community. Our typical American "Lone Ranger" individualism resists commitment to and sharing with others. Also, our overly busy lives in this ever-faster-moving world leave no time for "loving and being united to one another," to use St. Angela's words. But if we don't find a way to associate with others in some form of Christian community, we are depriving ourselves of a significant source of support and life-empowering strength. As Pope Francis says, "Contrary to the growing consumerist individualism that tends to isolate us in a quest for well-being apart from others, our path to holiness can only make us identify all the more with Jesus' prayer 'that all may be one; even as you, Father, are in me, and I in you.'" [1]

As you read St. Angela's story, I encourage you to reflect on the importance of community for drawing nearer to God and for living an effective Christian life.

Like St. Catherine of Siena and numerous other holy women, St. Angela Merici possessed a charismatic charm that attracted people. A lovely woman with an engaging personality, she related freely with women and men from all levels of society, making friends both among both the wealthy and the poor. From her early twenties she welcomed young women who came to her for advice and support. Some gathered around her in an informal community and shared her work of spreading the Catholic faith to children. Late in her life she organized her associates into a band of committed women that ultimately developed into the Company of St. Ursula.

Angela Merici was born at Desenzano, near Lake Garda in Lombardy, northern Italy, in 1474. Her father was a wealthy farmer and her mother a member of the lesser nobility, which would later help her gain access to influential people. We know little about Angela's childhood, except that the Mericis were apparently a close-knit, devout Catholic family. For example, her father read saints' lives to the children every evening from Jacob Voragine's *Golden Legend,* one of the fifteenth century's best-selling books. So perhaps while Angela cuddled on her father's lap at age five, the legend of St. Ursula and her army of eleven thousand heroic virgin martyrs captivated her imagination and initiated her lifelong devotion to the saint.[2] Three brothers, a sister, and her parents died when Angela was young, leaving her and a sister as orphans. Her uncle brought them to his home at Salò on Lake Como and cared for them in his family.

Angela's mission began to take shape in her teen years, first through her decision to join the Third Order of St. Francis, and second, through a vision she received.

St. Francis of Assisi had founded the Third Order in 1221 for lay men and women who wanted to live according to the ideals of his first and second orders, the Friars Minor and the Poor Clares. He drafted a rule that directed members to live a simple, penitent lifestyle. He required that they wear a rough habit, avoid secular entertainments, pray the Liturgy of the Hours or other prayers, adopt a regimen of fasting, and devote themselves to Christian service. Tertiaries, as they were called, committed themselves to go to confession and receive Holy Communion three times a year, which was normal practice in the thirteenth-century church. They lived with their families at home and gathered once a month for teaching, study, spiritual direction, and personal sharing.[3]

Angela likely was attracted to the Third Order because by the fifteenth century members were allowed the then-uncommon practice of frequent Communion.[4] So at Salò she embraced the Franciscan ideals enthusiastically. For the rest of her life she wore a simple gray habit and was called "Sister Angela." While no direct evidence connects Angela's experience of the Third Order with the pattern of life she later gave to her community of women, it undoubtedly influenced her in shaping it.[5]

In her late teens or early twenties, Angela experienced a vision that revealed her vocation and set the course of her life. One day while visiting a farm on the road from Desenzano to Salò, she stopped to pray at a secluded spot called Brudazzo. As she prayed she saw a vast number of young women, each paired with an angel, descending from the sky to the earth. The maidens were singing a song, accompanied by the angels. Angela recognized one of the women as her beloved sister, who had recently died. The procession stopped, and her sister told Angela that God wanted her to found a company of thousands of virgins, whose ministry would extend into the distant future.[6] Angela believed that in the vision God had given her a blueprint of what she was supposed to do with her life. For the next forty years, with practical wisdom and prudence, she associated with numerous young women, expecting that the Holy Spirit would show her how and when to form the community predicted in the vision.

Angela's uncle died when she was twenty-two, and she returned from Salò to Desenzano. She lived for a time with an aristocratic widow, who introduced her to people of influence in the towns around Lake Garda. She developed friendships with men and women who were drawn to her because of her obvious holiness. As her Christian service for the Third Order, Angela dedicated herself to educating children in the faith. Other young women, some from the Third Order and some from all social levels, including the lower classes, joined her in her catechetical work. Her spiritual influence became the glue that bound them together as a support group for unmarried young women in their neighborhoods.[7]

At the invitation of aristocratic friends, Angela moved to Brescia in 1516. She came to believe that God wanted her to organize her company of virgins in this major cultural center. Social conditions in Brescia, however, had deteriorated severely. From 1494 through 1531, the French, the Spanish, and the Emperor Charles V had ravaged the city in turn. Amid dangers and disruptions, Angela exercised her gift for friendship to develop relationships among the rich and the poor and worked to restore peace among leaders of warring factions. As she had done in the lake country, she gathered young women into a loose association of catechists. But she waited patiently for the right time to launch her community.

In 1525 Angela took a major step toward implementing her youthful vision. She made a pilgrimage to Rome, where she discussed with Pope Clement VII her ideas for a company of virgins who would serve in the world. Apparently the pope blessed Angela's plan in principle but did not give her written approval.[8] The political and social turmoil in beleaguered Brescia prevented her from moving forward until 1530. Then she began holding occasional meetings for prayer and teaching with the women who had involved themselves in her work. She instructed them in Christian living, sharing her ideals and vision with them.

In 1534 Angela began to hold regular meetings of women she regarded as candidates to form the nucleus of her community. They met at the house of a wealthy widow in a room decorated with murals of Christ's life and of saints, including Ursula, Paula (347–404), a famous disciple of St. Jerome (c. 341–420), and Elizabeth of Hungary (1207–1231), who served as appropriate patronesses for the group.[9] Finally, on November 25, 1534, the feast of St. Catherine of Alexandria (d. c. 310), the patroness of virgins, Angela formally organized the Company of Saint Ursula. Twenty-eight women embraced the principles that she promulgated, although she would not have a written rule until 1536.

THE PATTERN FOR COMMUNITY LIFE
SAINT PAUL (FIRST CENTURY)

St. Paul taught that a Christian community is the Body of Christ, with each member contributing his gifts for the life of all.

Just as each of us has various parts in one body, and the parts do not all have the same function: in the same way, all of us, though there are so many of us, make up one body in Christ, and as different parts we are all joined to one another. Then since the gifts that we have differ according to the grace that was given to each of us: if it is a gift of prophecy, we should prophesy as much as our faith tells us; if it is a gift of practical service, let us devote ourselves to serving; if it is teaching, to teaching; if it is encouraging, to encouraging.

When you give, you should give generously from the heart; if you are put in charge, you must be conscientious; if you do works of mercy, let it be because you enjoy doing them. Let love be without any pretense. Avoid what is evil; stick to what is good. In brotherly love let your feelings of deep affection for one another come to expression and regard others as more important than yourself. In the service of the Lord, work not halfheartedly but with conscientiousness and an eager spirit. Be joyful in hope, persevere in hardship; keep praying regularly; share with any of God's holy people who are in need; look for opportunities to be hospitable.

—Romans 12:4–13

Angela gave her sisters a pattern of life that reflected her own spirituality and experience in the Third Order of St. Francis. She wanted the company to have enough structure to ensure that the members would adhere to her ideals, but enough freedom so that they could follow the leadings of the Holy Spirit.[10] Members of her company would not take vows, but would promise to remain virgins. They would be committed to common ideals of life and service but live at home with their families. They would practice a fixed regimen of prayer and fasting. The sisters would dress simply, but not wear a habit. They would limit their contacts with worldly culture. The members would meet every first Friday for prayer, instruction, sharing, and spiritual direction.

Angela's creative application of such Third Order principles to a community of women departed radically from the tradition of removing women religious entirely from the world and enclosing them in cloisters. Her sisters would be in the world, but not of it, serving the Lord and the church by catechizing children. Angela guaranteed the spiritual health of the community members by devising a system of government in which mature women cared for and guided them.

Angela established other principles that had revolutionary consequences. She required that applicants to her community enter "gladly and of their own free will."[11] Thus the company would not become a haven for wealthy families to relegate unmarriageable and unhappy daughters. Also Angela leveled class distinctions within the community, tolerating no favoritism for noble or aristocratic women.[12] These requirements, which departed from both religious and social traditions, strengthened the company by removing obstacles to peaceful and loving relationships.

Angela had designed an avant-garde community that benefited its members, their families, and the local society. Not only did she provide a solid spiritual life for her sisters, but she also established a system that protected them socially, especially those from the lower classes. In an age when poor women could easily be forced into menial service or prostitution, Angela's community, in effect, created a social class of virgins. She revived the ancient Christian practice of honoring women who chose to remain unmarried in the service of Christ and the church.[13] So she gave her sisters both social status and self-respect.

Angela had her community members live at home so that their witness would have a transforming effect on their families.[14] She required the sisters to obey their parents or guardians, which pleased family members and made them more open to imitating the spirituality of the company. Consequently, family members were drawn back to the church, entered into closer relationships with God, and began to pray and worship at daily Mass.

EVANGELIZING WITH LOVE AND HOLINESS

A community that cherishes the little details of love, whose members care for one another and create an open and evangelizing environment, is a place where the risen Lord is present, sanctifying it in accordance with the Father's plan.
—POPE FRANCIS, *Rejoice and Be Glad*, 145

And Angela expected her sisters to Christianize the local culture through their life in their families and their education of children in the faith. She counseled community leaders to ensure that the young women always behaved in a Christian manner:

I want [the sisters] to give good example wherever they are, so that they may be to all a fresh fragrance of virtue, obedient and submissive to their superiors, seeking to spread peace and harmony. Above all, let them be unassuming and kind, let all their behavior, either in word or deed, be marked with charity, and let them bear everything with patience.[15]

Like all healthy Christian groups, the Company of St. Ursula strengthened its members so that they could focus their energy and service on the people in their social environments.

By the time St. Angela Merici died in 1540, her Company of St. Ursula was well on the way to establishing itself as a unique religious community devoted to the Christian education of girls and young women. Her charism was a gift for teaching women, and her genius was the ability to shape her work to meet the social and religious needs of her age. The saint's work has stood the test of time. The Ursulines, while they have undergone considerable changes, have fulfilled Angela's vision and have extended her ministry of education through more than five centuries.

You may be wondering what a sixteenth-century community of virgins has to do with twenty-first-century Catholic laypeople. The relevance lies in the importance St. Angela placed on community as an essential ingredient of the Christian life, and in the key elements of community living that she established in the rule of the Company of St. Ursula. Pope Francis affirms this view in *The Joy of the Gospel*: "At the very heart of the Gospel is life in community and engagement with others."[16] I admire St. Angela's grasp of the indispensable role community plays in keeping Christians close to the Lord. She pioneered the formation of groups that enable laypeople to live a disciplined spiritual life in the world. She paved the way for a great diversity of modern lay associations—secular institutes, fraternities, sodalities, covenant communities, and prayer groups—that have renewed and empowered the contemporary church. Over the past five decades, my participation in such groups has supported me and made me a stronger, more faithful Christian. If I had tried to go it alone, independent of brothers and sisters, I would have missed out on the fullness of the Christian life that God intends for us, his family.

Twenty-first-century Catholics and other Christians must find ways of creating Christian communities that both support their members and reach out to serve the needs of others. We must imitate the women of Angela's company and come together in groups committed to the ideals of love and service. And we must imitate the practices Angela required of her members that fit our situations: a common regimen of prayer and study, a commitment to work together toward common goals, a duty to support one another spiritually and materially, and the privilege of sharing the good news with others.

Think, Pray, and Act

Reflect on your experience of Christian community in your parish or in some group, perhaps a religious movement or social organization.

Think

🏃 In what ways have I experienced Christian community?

🏃 Have I participated in a small group in my parish? A faith-sharing group? A Bible study group? A service team? Other?

🏃 Have I participated in a community group in a religious organization or movement? A Third Order? The Cursillo? Prayer group? Other?

- If so, what was my experience like? How did participation benefit me? If not, what might be the benefit to me of participating in such a group?

Pray

- Take half an hour to reflect on the nature and value of Christian community. Read Acts 2:46–47, which describes the earliest Christian community. What do these verses seem to be saying to you about your participation in community?

- Ask the Holy Spirit for guidance about the possibility of getting involved with some Christian community group.

Act

- As an experiment in Christian community, invite eight or nine friends to participate in a nine-week Bible study. Use Rich Cleveland, *Living in the Power of the Holy Spirit: A Catholic Bible Study,* which is available from The Word Among Us (www.wordamongus.org; 800-775-9673). If you decide the community experience was valuable, plan to continue meeting.

May you look for ways of connecting with sisters and brothers in communal relationships in your family, parish, friendships, and neighborhood. And may your experience of Christian community advance you in holiness.

Seven SOCIAL JUSTICE
Saint Roque González (1576–1628)

Let no one take it ill that in the light of God's words read in our Mass we enlighten social, political, and economic realities. If we did not, it would not be Christianity for us. It is thus that Christ willed to become incarnate, so that the light that he brings from the Father may become the light of men and of nations.[1]

—Blessed Oscar Romero (1917–1980)

Those who really wish to give glory to God by their lives, who truly long to grow in holiness, are called to be single-minded and tenacious in their practice of the works of mercy.

—Pope Francis, *Rejoice and Be Glad,* 107

My study of the lives of the saints has taught me that these are marks of authentic spirituality:

The nearer you draw to God, the nearer you draw to others.

The better you come to know God, the better you know the needs of others.

The more you love God, the more you love others.

The more spiritual you become, the more active you become in serving others.

These principles hold true because as we open our hearts to God, he opens his heart to us. He reveals to us his passionate concern for the well-being of his beloved human beings, and he presses us to care for them in his behalf. As he showed in Scripture, he especially calls us to serve people with great needs—orphans, widows, strangers, migrants, the sick, and the poor. He wants those who have wealth,

*resources, and power to use them to support those who have none
of these things.*

*Today we use the term "social justice" to name the divinely
inspired impulse to act on behalf of marginalized people. The term
encompasses both one-on-one acts of service and corporate efforts to
change oppressive social, political, or economic institutions. Before
the term "social justice" was popularized in the twentieth century,
saints described their social justice activities as works of charity.
All saints performed personal service for people in need. And many
dedicated themselves to reforming or establishing institutions that
we now would call social justice initiatives. Of them, I think that
the life and accomplishments of St. Roque González may be most
inspiring and instructive.*

The first saints acclaimed by the church were martyrs. Local
Christian communities honored men and women who gave
their lives for the gospel because they were following Christ
perfectly by conforming to his death. Beginning with Luke's
account of the martyrdom of Stephen in Acts 6–7, Christian
writers celebrated the similarity of martyrs' deaths to Christ's
by carefully selecting details that resembled his passion and
crucifixion. It came to be expected that the lives of martyrs
would include events that marked Jesus' martyrdom, such as
confrontations with accusers or unbelievers, voices from heaven,
trials before religious or civil courts, false witnesses, beatings, and
mockery. And sometimes when the historical record left few facts
to work with, biographers used their imagination to fill the gaps.
They created legends to ensure that no one would fail to see how
closely their subject followed Christ in both life and death.

But the biographers of St. Roque González needed no fictions
to portray his likeness to Christ. For three decades, this great
seventeenth-century missionary and social activist laid down

his life daily for his beloved Guaraní people of Paraguay. Roque endured the hardships of traveling miles on foot through forests and bogs, extremes of heat and cold, the constant companionship of mosquitoes, plus exhaustion, hunger, disease, danger from wild animals and enemies, and opposition from Spanish landholders. Imitating his Master, he suffered all things, even death, in order to care for his people—to feed them, to heal their diseases, to free them from slavery, to bring them the gospel, and to gather them into Christian communities.

Roque González de Santa Cruz was born in 1576 at Asunción, the capital of Paraguay. His father, Bartolomé González, was a conquistador, one of the thousands of adventurers who, with the encouragement of Spain and Portugal, conquered and colonized the New World. Nothing is known about his mother, María de Santa Cruz, but some historians speculate that she may have been part Indian. Roque's family heritage provided him excellent credentials for his missionary work. Because Roque was a native-born Paraguayan, he did not bear fully the stigma of his descent from conquistadors, the hated European oppressors of the Indians. And from childhood he spoke the language of the Guaraní, possibly a gift from his mother that opened a natural relationship for him with the people he would ultimately serve.

By 1599, the year Roque was ordained a priest, the Spanish and Portuguese conquest of South America was nearly complete. Lust for gold, land, and power drove the conquistadors and, armed with guns and mounted on horses, their superior forces easily prevailed. Spain had enacted laws that safeguarded the natives' rights to their lands and prohibited slavery. At the same time Spain established the *encomienda* system as a way to encourage its people to settle in South America. Under this system, colonists and conquistadors were offered large land grants, to be held in trust for the indigenous people, who had been called "Indians" since the first Europeans mistakenly thought they had landed in the Indies.

THE ROOTS OF SLAVERY

Today, as in the past, slavery is rooted in a notion of the human person which allows him or her to be treated as an object. Whenever sin corrupts the human heart and distances us from our Creator and our neighbours, the latter are no longer regarded as beings of equal dignity, as brothers or sisters sharing a common humanity, but rather as objects. . . . [H]uman persons created in the image and likeness of God . . . are treated as means to an end.

—POPE FRANCIS, Message for the World Day of Peace, January 1, 2015

The *encomenderos* were supposed to protect the natives and arrange for their Christianization. In return, the natives were required to pay the *encomenderos* in the form of taxes and labor. But the system became corrupt very quickly. The *encomenderos* forced the Indians to perform day labor and treated them as slaves. And worse, Portuguese *bandierantes* from São Paulo, Brazil, captured thousands of Indians and sold them into slavery. For an accurate depiction of this hideous oppression of the Guaraní, you should view *The Mission*, even though the events depicted in this movie happened 150 years after Roque González's time. Recently, when I watched it, I was horrified at the brutal treatment of the natives that has persisted even to this day.

The greed and violence of the colonists obstructed the efforts of missionaries to attract the Indians to Christ and the church, and the oppression the missionaries witnessed made them advocates for social justice. A century before Roque González began his work, Bartolomé de Las Casas, a priest and an *encomendero,* was so touched by the abuses he witnessed that he renounced his land and freed his Indian slaves. Then he joined the Dominicans and became a passionate champion of justice for the Indians. For more than half a century he made numerous trips to the Spanish court to plead their cause to the king. In his appeals he identified their sufferings with those of Christ. Once he wrote, "I leave in the Indies Jesus Christ, our God, scourged and afflicted and beaten and crucified not once, but thousands of times."[2] The king of Spain did promulgate more humane laws, and as early as 1537 the pope condemned the enslavement of the Indians. But Madrid and Rome were thousands of miles from America, and the interventions of both king and pope were ignored.

For three years after his ordination, Roque González was deployed as a missionary to Mbaracayú, an area near Asunción inhabited by many conquered tribes that had been placed in the *encomienda* system. The people of Mbaracayú received him warmly. In the broadest sense of the Spanish verb *conquistar,* he "won over" many of them to Christianity with his gentle persuasiveness and service. He had come from conquistador roots, but all of his conquests were spiritual.[3]

In 1603, the bishop recalled Roque from his mission and appointed him as rector of the cathedral at Asunción. Historians hypothesize that powerful colonists pressed for Roque's removal from Mbaracayú because he actively opposed their enslavement of Indians to work on their tea plantations.[4] Over the next six years the bishop came to rely on the gifted young priest. But in 1609, when the bishop attempted to name Roque vicar-general of the diocese, he declined the position. Motivated by his missionary impulse and commitment to justice, he then joined the Jesuits, who were leaders in caring for the Indians.

The Jesuits were spearheading a significant, and now famous, social experiment in Paraguay. They were drawing the Guaraní, a large nomadic tribe, into a system of innovative communities called the *reducción de Indios.* Unfortunately, the word *reducción* leads to confusion because of its association with the word "reduction." Although the Spanish verb *reducir* normally meant "to reduce," in the mission field it had the technical meaning of "to gather into settled communities."[5] The Jesuit reductions were independent Indian villages, self-governing and economically self-contained.

Roque González was a pioneering architect of the reductions. In 1611 he established the reduction of San Ignacio Guazú, named for St. Ignatius of Loyola, the founder of the Jesuits. He located the settlement in a fertile and forested area between two rivers, the Tebicuary and the Paraná. In the following letter to his Jesuit superior in 1613, he described St. Ignacio, providing a typical picture of life in the reductions:

> The countryside near this little town is quite charming, and the climate is excellent, not nearly so apt to cause illness as are some other areas. The fields are fertile, widespread, and large enough to keep some four hundred farmers busy. There is no lack of water and firewood. Nearby forests offer opportunities for hunting, and all sorts of wild animals are plentiful. All this makes it easy for the Indians to forget about fishing, their main occupation in their homeland. . . . Last year there was already something of a harvest. This year there is an abundance, which makes the people very happy. In this town there are some three hundred families, and in the vicinity some four hundred others, enough for another town. . . .

This town had to be built from its very foundations. In order to do away with occasions of sin, I decided to build it in the style of the Spaniards, so that everyone should have his own house, with fixed boundaries and a corresponding yard. This system prevents easy access from one house to another, which used to be the case and which gave occasion for drunken orgies and other evils.

A church and rectory are being erected for our needs. Comfortable and enclosed with an adobe wall, the houses are built with cedar girders—cedar is very common wood here. We have worked hard to arrange all this. But with even greater zest and energy—in fact with all our strength—we have worked to build temples to Our Lord, not only those made by hands but spiritual temples as well, namely the souls of these Indians.

On Sundays and feast days we preach during mass, explaining the catechism beforehand with equal concern for boys and girls. The adults are instructed in separate groups of about 150 men and the same number of women. Shortly after lunch, we teach them reading and writing for about two hours.

There are still many non-Christians in this town. Because of the demands of planting and harvesting all cannot be baptized at the same time. So every month we choose those best prepared for baptism. Among the 120 or so adults baptized this year there were several elderly shamans.[6]

Influenced by Roque's design at St. Ignacio and subsequent foundations over twenty years, reductions were generally located near rivers or other fertile areas. The little towns were built around a central square with a church, rectory, a home for widows and orphans, offices, and a storehouse situated opposite the houses of the Indians. The economy of the reductions combined collective agriculture with private ownership—the Indians farmed the main crops together but maintained their own gardens and animals.[7] In these settlements the Jesuits provided for the spiritual and material needs of the Indians. They introduced them to Christ and the church, a primary missionary concern. But they also taught the Indians to read and write and trained them in skills and crafts, such as masonry, carpentry, painting, sculpture, and music.

To guarantee the freedom of the Guaraní and to protect their rights, Europeans were excluded from the reductions. The political autonomy of these settlements enraged the colonists and conquistadors. The *encomenderos* abhorred the reductions because they were safe havens for Indians. The settlements deprived them of labor and services to which they felt entitled. And they resented that the Jesuits had condemned the practices of the *encomienda* system as a form of slavery.

Roque courageously faced this angry opposition during all the years of his missionary service. In December 1614 he expressed his views in a bold letter to his brother Francisco, the lieutenant governor of Asunción, who sided with the *encomenderos:*

> I have received your letter and understand from it and from other letters the strong feeling and complaints you have regarding the Indians and especially the feelings you have against us.
>
> This is nothing new, nor anything that started yesterday. The *encomendero* gentlemen and soldiers have long complained and even gone further by stirring up strong opposition to the Society of Jesus. This, in fact, is a great honor to us.
>
> I say this because the cause of the Indians is so just and because they have and have had a right to be free from the harsh slavery and forced labor called *personal service.*

Indeed, they are exempt from this by natural law, both divine and human.

These complaints grew even more serious after members of the Society fulfilled their obligation as faithful ministers of God and vassals of his majesty the King and supported what he ordered most justly through his visitor that the Indians should be free from the servitude in which they were kept.[8]

Roque championed justice for the Indians without fear of his enemies. He took the offensive and attacked their arrogant behavior with a spiritual weapon, as he explained in the same letter to Francisco:

And because the *encomenderos* live in such a state of blindness, no God-fearing priest will hear their confessions. For my part I tell you that I will not hear the confession of any one of them, for anything in this world, because they have done evil and are not willing to admit it, much less to make restitution and amend their lives. In the next world their eyes will be opened, to their great distress, unless they mend their ways now and make up with Indians in the sight of him who is infinitely wise and cannot be deceived.[9]

If Francisco replied to Roque, his letter is lost. But we know that Roque's aggressive stance affected him. In February 1605, just two months after receiving his brother's blast, Francisco issued a document authorizing Roque and the Jesuits to set up "three or four" new reductions and forbad anyone to obstruct or impede their establishment.[10]

TENDER MERCIES

The works of mercy reawaken in us the need, and the ability, to make the faith alive and active with charity. These works of mercy are the features of the face of Jesus Christ, who takes care of his littlest brethren in order to bring the tenderness and closeness of God to each of them.

—Pope Francis, General Audience, October 12, 2016

During the dozen years from 1615 to 1627, Roque González established reductions in Paraguay, southern Brazil, northeastern Argentina, and Uruguay. He lived with the Indians he loved. He ate their food, lived in houses like theirs, and worked side by side with them building their towns and cultivating their fields. When their harvests failed, he starved with them until he could arrange for relief from other reductions. He personally tended them when they were sick. For the Guaraní, Roque González was advocate of their rights, pastor, physician, architect, builder, teacher, and agriculturalist. He shines as an exemplar of service evangelism: winning people to Christ by loving them and meeting their material needs.

In 1628 two young Jesuits, Juan de Castillo and Alonso Rodríguez, teamed up with Roque. On August 15 the three priests founded a reduction at the Ijuhi River in Paraguay, and dedicated it to Mary because the feast of the Assumption was celebrated on that day. Roque left Juan in charge, and he and Alonso went to Caaró, at the southern tip of Brazil. There, on November 1, they established a reduction and named it after that day's feast of All Saints. Their intrusion into these areas triggered the animosity of Nezú, a local medicine man, who decided to kill all the Jesuits in his territory. On November 15, one of Nezú's men surprised Roque from behind, killing him with a single blow. Then they killed Alonso and dragged both bodies into the chapel, which they set on fire. In the next few days, Nezú's henchmen murdered Juan de Castillo and three other Jesuits.

Like the Master he had followed faithfully, Roque González's life of selfless service ended in a bloody death.

GIVING RESPECT TO THE POOR
BLESSED FREDERIC OZANAM (1813–1853)

We should care for the poor in a way that honors them, so that they can reciprocate our gifts.

Help is humiliating when it appeals to men from below, taking heed only of their material wants. It humiliates when there is no reciprocity. When you give a poor man nothing but bread or clothes, there is no likelihood of his ever giving you anything in return.

But help honors when it appeals to him from above. It respects him when it deals with his soul, with his religious, moral and political education, and with all that emancipates him from his passions. Help honors when, to the bread that nourishes, it adds the visit that consoles, advice that enlightens, the friendly handshake that lifts up flagging courage. It esteems the poor man when it treats him with respect, not only as an equal, but as a superior, since he is suffering what perhaps we are incapable of suffering. After all, he is the messenger of God to us, sent to prove our justice and our charity, and to save us by our works.

Help then becomes honorable, because it may become mutual. Every person who gives a kind word, good advice, a consolation today, may tomorrow need a kind word, advice, or consolation. The hand that you clasp clasps yours in return. That indigent family whom you love loves you in return, and will have largely acquitted themselves towards you when they shall have prayed for you.

—Adapted from an October 21, 1848, article in Ozanam's newspaper, *New Era*, reprinted in *Frédéric Ozanam: His Life and Works*, by Kathleen O'Meara (New York: Christian Press Association Publishing Company, 1891).

Roque González played a key role in one of the most effective social justice movements in Christian history. The reductions thrived in South America for a hundred fifty years and collapsed only after Spain expelled the Jesuits in 1768. Over the years, 1,565 Jesuit priests and brothers worked in the Paraguayan province. They built more than thirty reductions, each housing two to four thousand Indians. By the time the Jesuits were expelled, the reductions were home to about eighty thousand people.[11]

Voltaire, the cynical voice of the Enlightenment, recognized the significant achievement of the Jesuits. He wrote,

> When the Paraguayan missions left the hands of the Jesuits in 1768, they had reached the highest degree of civilization to which it is possible to lead a young people. . . . In those missions, law was respected, morals were pure, a happy brotherliness bound men together, the useful arts and even some of the more graceful sciences flourished, and there was abundance everywhere.[12]

Some of us may be called to follow St. Roque and dedicate our lives to obtaining justice for marginalized people. But all of us, if we truly desire to become Spirit-filled women and men, must find ways to act in God's behalf for the poor, the sick, and the oppressed. Pope Francis encourages us with these words: "May the Holy Spirit help us; May the Holy Spirit kindle within us the desire to live this way of life: at least once a day, at least! Let us again learn the corporal and spiritual works of mercy by heart, and ask the Lord to help us put them into practice every day, and in those moments where we see Jesus in a person who is in need."[13]

Think, Pray, and Act

Take stock of the situations of people in your social environments—
your home, your neighborhood, your church, and your town. Use
the following questions to help you assess their needs and your
ability to serve them personally in some way.

Think

🏃 What person in my social environments has the greatest
need? It could be a family member or relative, a neighbor, a
parishioner, a single parent, a homeless person, or someone
who is sick or has a disability. What does this person need?
What is his or her greatest need?

🏃 Is there a social justice program, either in my parish or
local area, where I could volunteer my time? What skills or
experience could I bring to help those in need?

Pray

🏃 Take thirty minutes to prayerfully consider how you might
undertake some social justice action. Ask the Holy Spirit to
guide you. Consider whether you might have the ability and
resources to help someone in your social environment meet
a significant need.

🏃 Prayerfully consider the possibility of working with some
local program that aids poor or marginalized members of
the community.

Act

✹ Decide to take some action within the next two weeks to serve the needs of a person in your social environment. What will you do?

✹ Or decide to get involved for at least six weeks with a local social justice program. What will you join?

✹ When you have completed your action, write down what you learned.

May you perform one of the corporal or spiritual works of mercy every day. May you look for ways to work for social justice in your town. And may you serve the poor without self-concern.

Eight EVANGELIZATION
POPE SAINT JOHN PAUL II (1920–2005)

Go out to the whole world; proclaim the gospel to all creation.
—*Mark 16:15*

No believer in Christ . . . can avoid this supreme duty: to proclaim Christ to all peoples.
—POPE JOHN PAUL II, *The Mission of the Redeemer*, 3

Every Christian is challenged, here and now, to be actively engaged in evangelization; indeed, anyone who has truly experienced God's saving love does not need much time or lengthy training to go out and proclaim that love.
—POPE FRANCIS, *The Joy of the Gospel*, 120

Just before he ascended to his Father, Jesus gave his disciples his final instructions. "Go," he said, "make disciples of all nations" (Matthew 28:19). He carefully chose his last words to his friends in order to affirm the mission of the church that he was establishing among them. He wanted this declaration of purpose to stick in their minds and propel them to action. They took his command to heart. Immediately after they had received the Holy Spirit at Pentecost, they added some three thousand to their number (see Acts 2:41). Over the next several decades, the apostles proclaimed the good news throughout the world. Paul and his team carried the gospel throughout Greece and Asia Minor. Peter went west to Rome, Thomas south to India, and Andrew reputedly in many directions to Constantinople, Russia, and Scotland.

Over the centuries, other missionaries set their hearts on the work of evangelization. St. Patrick (387–461) and St. Brigid (c. 450–525) established monasteries that converted the people of Ireland, and St. Boniface (c. 680–754) and St. Leoba (d. 779) did the same for Germany and France. St. Francis of Assisi (1181–1226) and St. Dominic (1170–1221) founded religious orders that turned their worlds "upside right" with the gospel. The Jesuit St. Francis Xavier (1506–1552) made disciples from southern India to Japan. Other Jesuits like St. Roque González (1576–1628) and St. John de Brebeuf (1593–1649) took the good news to the natives of the Americas. In the mid-nineteenth century, two young French missionaries—Sts. Jean-Gabriel Perboyre (1802–1840) in China and Théophane Venard (1829–1861) in Indochina—gave their lives to win followers of Christ. I could continue to list disciple makers, but you get the idea.

All of these evangelizers belonged to either monastic communities or religious orders. But since the Second Vatican Council, the church has emphasized the responsibility of all Christians, especially laypeople, to lead others to Christ. "On all Christians," said the council fathers, "is laid the splendid burden of working to make the divine message of salvation known and accepted by all people throughout the world."[1] So the council reminded all Catholic laity of their privileged duty to undertake the work of evangelization. Popes Paul VI and John Paul II have repeatedly urged us to view spreading the gospel as the most important thing that we do.[2] And Pope Francis summed up our evangelistic responsibility in an expression that has become a watchword: "Every Christian is a missionary to the extent that he or she has encountered the love of God in Christ Jesus: we no longer say that we are 'disciples' and 'missionaries', but rather that we are always 'missionary disciples'. . . . So what are we waiting for?"[3]

However, most Catholic laypeople in the Western world do not seem to be doing much evangelizing. In my diocese of four hundred thousand Catholics, for example, only a thousand adults were baptized last year. Most of these joined the church primarily for

family reasons, not because one of us introduced them to Christ.
Why don't we get more involved in evangelization? I think the main
reason is ignorance of our duty to spread the gospel in spite of the
significant efforts of Vatican II and the popes to educate us.

Pope St. John Paul II not only told us that we must become
evangelizers, but he also showed us how to do it. Don't be put off
by comparing his global evangelization to our much smaller, local
endeavors. Even though his mission field was the whole world, John
Paul II's teaching and witness demonstrated how we can share the
gospel with our neighbors and influence for Christ the culture of our
worlds.

From the time of his election as pope in 1978, John Paul II
believed that God had appointed him to prepare the church for
the coming of the new millennium. At the opening of the twenty-
first century, the pope wanted to bring all into a springtime of
renewed faith, hope, and love. Among a multiplicity of initiatives
to make this happen, he focused his efforts on the church's singular
mission to offer the gift of salvation to all humanity. And to
generate this season of vibrant Christianity, John Paul II launched
a great project, which he called "the New Evangelization."

The New Evangelization did not replace the gospel of Christ
with a "new" message. The newness consisted in the way John Paul
II tailored the approach and scope of evangelization to respond
to the needs of the contemporary world. He based his strategy on
the teachings of Vatican II and Pope Paul VI and structured it into
four categories: involvement of all Catholics in evangelization; re-
evangelization of the church and the world; the Christianization of
culture; and participation of the laity in missionary activity.

In previous centuries the work of evangelization mainly fell to
men and women in monasteries and religious orders. Now the New
Evangelization placed a priority on calling all Catholics, especially

the laity, to embrace their responsibility to lead others to Christ and the church. "The lay faithful," wrote John Paul II, "precisely because they are members of the Church, have the vocation and mission of proclaiming the gospel."[4] He reckoned that laypeople who were immersed in secular environments were well positioned to communicate the Christian message to their contemporaries. He said that they must

> testify how the Christian faith constitutes the only fully valid response . . . to the problems and hopes that life poses to every person and society. This will be possible if the lay faithful will . . . overcome in themselves the separation of the gospel from life. . . .[5]

Thus, raising the awareness of the laity to their duty to evangelize became a major goal of his papacy.

In the second plank of the New Evangelization, John Paul II called for the re-evangelization of nations where Christianity had once flourished, but where faith had since dried up and withered. Large numbers of Westerners seem to have substituted the stuff of consumerism and the hollow values of secularism for the genuine spiritual benefits of the Christian faith. Even the church itself must be targeted for re-evangelization, for many of its members have not responded with conviction to Christ and the gospel. So John Paul II commissioned faithful laypersons to take on the task of revitalizing the commitment of nominal Christians among their fellows and their neighbors. "The present situation," he wrote, "not only of the world but of many parts of the Church, *absolutely demands that the word of Christ receive a more ready and generous obedience.*"[6]

The third plank of the New Evangelization called for the transformation of entire cultures. The pope saw the laity taking a lead in the process of making Christ present in the diverse ways people conduct their daily lives. He called on laypeople to be present as signs of courage and intellectual creativity in areas such as education, scientific and technological research, and the arts. Such a presence is destined, he said, for the elevation of these cultures through the riches that spring from the gospel and the Christian faith.[7]

He also commissioned lay leaders to present Christian values via the mass media. The New Evangelization required new communication vehicles to transmit the Christian message to the ends of the earth, and the pope called on laypeople to develop the expertise to do it well in print and electronic venues. As we will see, John Paul II himself mastered the art of using radio and television to proclaim the good news.

Pope John Paul II had a special concern for the millions throughout the world who had not heard the good news. As the twentieth century closed, missionary activity seemed to be waning, and the pope appealed to the whole church to revive it.[8] So he made increasing the participation of all Catholics in the church's missionary thrust the fourth element in the New Evangelization. The pope saw a special role for laypeople in the mission field, and he urged more of us to uproot ourselves, even if only for a short time, to carry the gospel to people who do not know Christ.[9]

The pope realized that his great evangelization project required that the evangelizers themselves respond to the gospel and make a commitment to Christ. "The New Evangelization," he said, "begins with the clear and emphatic proclamation of the gospel, which is directed to every person. Therefore it is necessary to awaken again in believers a full relationship with Christ, mankind's only Savior. Only from a personal relationship with Jesus can an effective evangelization develop."[10] For the twenty-seven years of his papacy, by his word and witness, John Paul II daily invited all to meet the Lord and come to know him. "Fall in love with Jesus

Christ," he said, "to live his very life, so that our world may have life in the light of the gospel."[11]

In his youth, Karol Wojtyla, the future Pope John Paul II, appeared on the stage, acting in plays that he had written and produced. As pope he took the church and the world as his stage and gave dramatic witness to Christ in a great diversity of ways. He had a knack for magnifying the impact of his actions, and he exploited this gift to its fullest. Telling the complete story of his evangelistic efforts would fill a hefty book, as it did in George Weigel's *Witness to Hope*.[12] I have chosen here to describe only a few of his initiatives that illustrate his personal implementation of the New Evangelization: his appeal to the young in his World Youth Days, his encounter with his would-be assassin, and his culturally revolutionary pilgrimage to Poland in 1979.

Pope John Paul II ignited rapport with young people in the early years of his papacy. For example, on his first visit to the United States in October 1979, he wooed tens of thousands of teenagers at Madison Square Garden in New York City. With school bands blaring popular music, he rode the "popemobile" up and down the aisles, greeting the kids and touching their outstretched hands. A riot of cheers echoed in the hall. At one point the youth began to chant, "John Paul II, we love you!" The pope, smiling broadly, responded with, "Woo-hoo-woo, John Paul II, he loves you."[13] This cheer sums up one reason why young people rallied around him: he won their affection because they could feel his love for them.

Karol Wojtyla discovered his charism for relating to youth early in his priesthood. He served as a chaplain to university students in Krákow. He invited these young men and women to join him at weekday Masses, gave them conferences, and took them hiking

SHOW AND TELL
Pope Saint Paul VI (1897–1978)

Our evangelization must involve more than setting a good example. We must speak to others about the good news and our testimony.

Above all the Gospel must be proclaimed by witness. Take a Christian or a handful of Christians who, in the midst of their own community, show their capacity for understanding and acceptance, their sharing of life and destiny with other people, their solidarity with the efforts of all for whatever is noble and good. Let us suppose that, in addition, they radiate in an altogether simple and unaffected way their faith in values that go beyond current values, and their hope in something that is not seen and that one would not dare to imagine. Through this wordless witness these Christians stir up irresistible questions in the hearts of those who see how they live: Why are they like this? Why do they live in this way? What or who is it that inspires them? Why are they in our midst? Such a witness is already a silent proclamation of the Good News and a very powerful and effective one. Here we have an initial act of evangelization. . . .

Nevertheless this always remains insufficient, because even the finest witness will prove ineffective in the long run if it is not explained, justified—what Peter called always having "your answer ready for people who ask you the reason for the hope that you all have" (see 1 Peter 3:15)—and made explicit by a clear and unequivocal proclamation of the Lord Jesus. The Good News proclaimed by the witness of life sooner or later has to be proclaimed by the word of life. There is no true evangelization if the name, the teaching, the life, the promises, the kingdom and the mystery of Jesus of Nazareth, the Son of God are not proclaimed.

—Pope St. Paul VI, Apostolic Exhortation, *Evangelii Nuntiandi* (On Evangelization in the Modern World), 21 and 22, at http//www.vatican.va.

and kayaking. Gradually, an informal community of young people formed around the future pope, sharing their lives with him. He was able to lead them to Christ and help them develop a modern Catholic lifestyle.[14] He called this group his "Środowisko," which meant his "accompaniment," and they became his lifelong friends. As Pope John Paul II looked back on the days of his Środowisko, his vision for World Youth Days was born. He realized that if he could accompany a small group of university students, he could also accompany the youth of the world and become their friend.[15]

THE ART OF ACCOMPANIMENT

In a culture paradoxically suffering from anonymity and at the same time obsessed with the details of other people's lives, the Church must look more closely and sympathetically at others whenever necessary. The Church will have to initiate everyone—priests, religious and laity—into this "art of accompaniment" which teaches us to remove our sandals before the sacred ground of the other (cf. Ex 3:5). The pace of this accompaniment must be steady and reassuring, reflecting our closeness and our compassionate gaze which also heals, liberates and encourages growth in the Christian life.

—POPE FRANCIS, *The Joy of the Gospel,* 169

In 1985 a quarter million young people gathered around him in Rome, and youth in dioceses throughout the world celebrated the first official World Youth Day (WYD) in 1986. Then the pope invited youth biennially to WYDs with him at international sites, beginning in 1987 at Buenos Aires. In alternate years, dioceses everywhere sponsored WYDs. Millions of young people from all over the world attended these joyous international celebrations. In fact, the closing Mass of the 1995 WYD in Manila drew five to seven million people, probably the largest gathering in human history.[16]

Pope John Paul II earned the confidence of youth because he took them seriously. They sensed that he understood their concerns. He challenged them to give their lives to Christ. He appealed to their high ideals, inviting them to take a lead in the New Evangelization. His message for the 1995 WYD typified his approach to young people. First, he reminded them that the Lord had touched their lives and urged them to continue to seek him in earnest prayer. Then he called on them to collaborate with him in proclaiming the gospel:

> You, young people, are especially called to become missionaries of this New Evangelization, by daily witnessing to the Word that saves. You personally experience the anxieties of the present historical period, fraught with hope and doubt, in which it can at times be easy to lose the way that leads to the encounter with Christ. . . . The Church entrusts to young people the task of proclaiming to the world the joy which springs from having met Christ. Dear friends, allow yourselves to be drawn to Christ, accept his invitation to follow him. Go and preach the Good News that redeems; do it with happiness in your hearts and become *communicators of hope* in a world which is often tempted to despair, *communicators of faith* in a society which at times seems resigned to disbelief, *communicators of love,* in daily events that are often marked by a mentality of the most unbridled selfishness.[17]

With such heart-to-heart communication, the pope created a dynamic friendship with millions of youth. Few if any of us will have opportunities to influence so many people for Christ and the church. But John Paul II's example teaches us the important lesson that making friends is the prerequisite to all evangelization.

On May 13, 1981, John Paul II nearly died from a would-be assassin's bullet. The pope's words and actions in response to this incident show us the importance of our witnessing to supernatural realities, especially the way God cares for our lives.

That day, as the pope was circling St. Peter's Square in the popemobile and greeting the crowd assembled for his general audience, Mehmet Ali Agca, a self-styled Turkish terrorist, shot him. He fired twice from a distance of about ten feet and hit the pope in the stomach. John Paul II was rushed to a nearby hospital, bleeding profusely and murmuring repeatedly, "Mary, my mother!"[18] Later the pope told a journalist that "at the very moment I fell in St. Peter's Square, I had this vivid presentiment that I should be saved, and this certainty never left me, even at the worst moments."[19] After five hours of surgery, the doctors announced that the beloved pope would survive. Four days later he sent a taped message to be played in St. Peter's Square. He said,

> I pray for that brother of ours who shot me, and whom I have sincerely pardoned. United with Christ, Priest and Victim, I offer my sufferings for the Church and for the world. Mary, I repeat: *Totus tuus, ego sum* (Mary, I am totally yours).[20]

John Paul II believed that the assassination attempt providentially occurred on the anniversary of Mary's appearance to the children at Fatima. He was convinced that because of Mary's intercession God had intervened to save him. "One hand fired," he said, "and another guided the bullet."[21] Any fair-minded observer must admit, at least, that something extraordinary, if not supernatural, had happened. A trained assassin had fired at close range, and the bullet sideswiped a main abdominal artery, missing it by a fraction of an inch.[22] The pope did not believe in accidents but held that God directed the flow of all human events, allowing things to happen and influencing outcomes. One year after the attempted assassination, he made a pilgrimage to Fatima to give thanks to God and Mary for protecting him. When he arrived there he expressed his conviction that his survival was no mere coincidence. George Weigel made this observation about John Paul II's visit to Fatima and his belief in Divine Providence:

> The assassination attempt, the fact that it took place on the date of the first Marian apparition at Fatima, the reasons it took place, his survival—none of this was an accident, just as the other incidents of his life, including his election to the papacy, had not been accidents. And this, he believed, was true of everyone. The world, including the world of politics, was caught up in the drama of God's saving purposes in history. That, to his mind, was the message the Second Vatican Council wanted to take to a modern world frightened by what seemed to be a purposelessness of life. The Church's primary task was to tell the world the story of its redemption, whose effects were working themselves out, hour by hour, in billions of lives in which there were no "mere coincidences."[23]

In the aftermath of his near-fatal attack, Pope John Paul II's witness showed us the way to testify to God's involvement in our lives. An exemplar of the New Evangelization himself, he wanted to demonstrate how to announce to our worlds that God was on the move in us, bringing justice to all. So he forgave his assailant and reconciled with him on a visit to his prison cell in December 1983. His example nudges us to bear witness to God's grace at work in us by forgiving those who hurt us. And his conversations about "no accidents, no coincidences" impel us to communicate to others how a loving God has their lives in his hands.

In June 1979 Pope John Paul II made a revolutionary pilgrimage to his native Poland. For nine days he conducted an evangelistic crusade across the nation, calling millions of his fellow countrymen to stand united as Christians against the Communist dictatorship that ruled them. At least thirteen million Poles saw John Paul in person, and virtually all of Poland's thirty-eight million people viewed him on television or heard him on radio. From the very first day of his visit, they caught his vision that God would work through them to reverse the course of history and restore their Christian nation.

John Paul II had timed his visit to correspond with the celebration of the thousandth anniversary of the martyrdom of St. Stanislaus (c. 1030–1079), who had died at the hands of a tyrannical king. Upon his arrival in Warsaw on June 2, the pope immediately electrified the nation by declaring that the election of a Polish pope was no accident. He said that God had chosen him at this moment in history because Poland had become a land with a responsibility to bear witness to religious freedom.[24] The entire nation got the message: just as St. Stanislaus had resisted the despotism of an autocratic state power, together they could resist the Communist state that oppressed them. He concluded his remarks with a challenge: "If we accept all that I dared to affirm in this moment, how many great duties and obligations arise? Are we capable of them?" The crowd spoke for all of Poland, chanting, "We want God! We want God!"[25]

The next day, the pope traveled to Gniezno, the birthplace of St. Adalbert (956–997), who is credited with the conversion of Poland.

There, a million people gathered around John Paul at an open-air Mass to celebrate the feast of Pentecost. The pope capitalized on the significance of both the day and the location of the event. On this Pentecost, he told the crowd, they were celebrating the birth of the Catholic Church in Poland. At the first Pentecost, thousands heard the apostles' message in their own tongues; now, millions of Slavic peoples were hearing in their own languages of Poland's opportunity to reclaim its religious freedom.[26]

Once again, John Paul II announced that God had chosen a Polish pope for this moment in history. But this time, he said, God arranged his election not only to revive the Polish nation, but also to manifest the spiritual unity of Christian Europe. Everyone understood that he was declaring void the post-World-War-II division of Eastern Europe into petty states. Instead, the pope urged all Slavic peoples to embrace their Christian cultural unity that transcended nation-states and military blocs. He promised them that God would usher them into a bright future. "This pope," he said, "blood of your blood, bone of your bone, will sing with you, and with you he will exclaim: 'May the glory of the Lord endure forever.' We shall not return to the past. We shall go forward to the future."[27]

From June 4 to 6, John Paul II repeated these themes in his messages at Częstochowa. At Mass at the famous shrine of the Black Madonna, he asked a million people to join him in entrusting the freedom of the church and the world to Mary, renewing the consecration of Poland to the Virgin that they had made on the occasion of the national millennium in 1966. He also urged the bishops of Poland not only to cultivate the revived cultural awareness of the Polish people, but also to champion the Christian cultural unity of Europe.

John Paul II carefully designed his homilies and addresses to awaken the Christian convictions of his listeners. He wanted to excite them with the possibility of their standing together as Christians against their oppressors. He achieved his goal on the first day of his pilgrimage and built on it the rest of the week. Millions of Poles had come to realize that they were not a Communist country, but a Christian nation saddled with a Communist state.[28] But the pope had to measure his words and temper the crowds in order not to incite them to violent demonstrations that would invite the state to intervene.

One event that had the potential of exploding into a riot against the government occurred in Warsaw on the evening of Friday, June 7. The pope was scheduled to address tens of thousands of young people, but he abandoned his prepared remarks, apparently sensing that their mounting enthusiasm could quickly escalate into a demonstration. Instead he bantered with the youth, joked with them, and joined their songs. At one point several young men raised a twelve-foot cross and tens of thousands raised smaller crosses, all seeming ready to stage an antigovernment protest. But the pope calmed them. "It's late, my friends," he said. "Let's go home quietly."[29] And they dispersed without incident.

John Paul II's pilgrimage climaxed on Sunday, June 10, when three million people assembled for Mass in Kraków Commons. In a little over a week he had generated a gentle but effective cultural revival in his home country. He told his vast congregation, both those present and those attending via television and radio, that in the great tradition of St. Stanislaus they were primed to make significant choices that would shape their future. He assured them that the Holy Spirit would be with them and guide their steps. He said, "You must be strong,"

dear brothers and sisters . . . You must be strong with the strength of *faith*. . . . You must be strong with the strength of *hope*, hope that brings the perfect joy of life and does not allow us to grieve the Holy Spirit. You must be strong with *love,* which is stronger than death. . . . and helps us to set up the great dialogue with man and the world rooted in the dialogue with God Himself, . . . the dialogue of salvation. . . . I beg you: never lose your trust, do not be defeated, do not be discouraged . . . and always seek spiritual power from Him whom countless generations of our fathers and mothers have found it. Never detach yourself from Him. Never lose your spiritual freedom . . . All this I beg of you.[30]

The New Evangelization charges laypeople with transforming their culture by living out the requirements of the gospel in all of their social environments. However, Pope John Paul II's example may seem too big, too daunting for us to imitate, his effort resembling a movie on an Imax screen and ours a pencil sketch on a notepad. Even so, we must consider making choices that allow God to act through us to care for others. For example, I meet regularly with a group of men involved in different services that make a cultural difference. Two of the men regularly volunteer to build houses for homeless people; one man counsels and supports relatives of people in prison; another man, a deacon, leads in our parish, preaching, giving spiritual direction, and, in addition, working with local police to help the victims of crime; and still another is a teacher who sets a high professional example among his peers. You get the picture. We need to behave in ways that show that God is working to set things right in our worlds. Just like Pope John Paul II—on a small scale, perhaps, but following his example nonetheless.

At the turn of the twentieth century, Pope John Paul's health declined severely. Parkinson's reduced his stamina, slowed his gait to a shuffle, and slurred his speech. He did not hide his disabilities, but allowed the public a full view of his illness. When someone asked him if he might retire because he had trouble walking and his hands trembled, he quipped, "Fortunately, I don't run the church with my hands or my feet, but with my mind."[31] The pope regarded his infirmities as a witness, modeling endurance and encouraging us by his example to face suffering with faith and peace.

THE POWER OF SUFFERING

Christ does not explain in the abstract the reasons for suffering, but before all else he says: "Follow me!" Come! Take part through your suffering in this work of saving the world. . . . Gradually, as the individual takes up his *cross*, spiritually uniting himself to the Cross of Christ, the salvific meaning of suffering is revealed before him.

—POPE JOHN PAUL II, *On the Christian Meaning of Suffering,* 26

The pope continued to govern the church faithfully until his disease took its final toll. Pope John Paul II died on April 2, 2005. Pope Francis canonized him along with Pope John XXIII on April 27, 2014.

Think, Pray, and Act

"How often we are tempted to keep close to the shore!" says Pope Francis. "Yet the Lord calls us to put out into the deep and let down our nets (cf. Lk 5:4). He bids us spend our lives in his service. Clinging to him, we are inspired to put all our charisms at the service of others. May we always feel compelled by his love (2 Cor 5:14) and say with Saint Paul: 'Woe to me if I do not preach the Gospel' (1 Cor 9:16)."[32] So, examine your life to determine how you might more effectively fulfill your duty and privilege to lead others to Christ and the church. Use the following questions to evaluate your involvement in evangelization and to determine how you might do more to proclaim the gospel in word and action.

Think

- How have I behaved in ways that attract people to Christ and the church? List some examples.

- How can I better recognize opportunities to share with others the reasons for my faith in Christ and the church? What holds me back? What have I said in the past, or what should I say now?

- Is there an evangelism team or training program in my parish? If so, how might I get involved? If not, how can I start one?

- Does my diocese offer any short-term missionary opportunities for laypeople? Have I ever considered undertaking a short-term missionary commitment? Why or why not?

⚕ In what ways do I contribute to influencing my culture and social environment for Christ and the church?

Pray

⚕ Take half an hour to pray quietly. Ask the Holy Spirit to suggest ways that you might get more involved in the New Evangelization.

Act

⚕ Review all your possibilities for participating in the New Evangelization. Select a way that fits well with your life and schedule and decide to do it for a month. At the end of the period, evaluate your evangelization and determine what you might do to improve it or add to it.

May you count on the Holy Spirit to equip you with the gifts you need to do the work of evangelization. May you pray for opportunities to share your faith with others and take the occasions to do it. And may you experience the joy of helping others give themselves more fully to God.

Nine PERSEVERANCE
SAINT JANE DE CHANTAL (1572–1641)

Contradictions, sickness, scruples, spiritual aridity, and all the inner and outward torments are the chisel with which God carves his statues for paradise.
—ST. ALPHONSUS LIGUORI (1696–1787)

For I am sure that neither death, nor life, nor angels, nor principalities, nor things present, nor things to come, nor powers, nor height, nor depth, nor anything else in all creation, will be able to separate us from the love of God in Christ Jesus our Lord.
—*Romans 8:38–39 (RSV)*

Solid grounding in the God who loves and sustains us . . . enables us to persevere amid life's ups and downs, but also to endure hostility, betrayal and failings on the part of others.
—POPE FRANCIS, *Rejoice and Be Glad,* 112

As a spiritual seeker you surely have bumped into popular gurus who guarantee an end to all suffering if you embrace their teaching. "Make these four agreements," says one, "and you will insulate yourself against adversity." Another says, "Focus on the power of now and still the persistent, evil voice of your thoughts. Then, you will never again experience pain or hardship." "Pray this arcane prayer religiously," says a third, "and it will ensure your comfort." The purveyors of these promises package their alluring messages attractively, and the books that convey them ascend to the top of the best-seller lists.

If you have tried their recipes, you may have discovered that for some reason they do not work for you. No matter how diligently you may keep the agreements, or try to focus on the now, or repeat the prayer formula, you still suffer trials, hardships, and pain. You may wonder why the magic of the gurus doesn't work for you. You may have concluded that somehow you missed their disclaimers that said you do not meet the requirements necessary to receive their promised benefits.

But the reason that these popular guarantees against suffering fail has nothing to do with you. They cannot deliver their promises because they are true neither to the human condition nor to authentic spirituality. A quick survey of family and friends should be enough to convince anyone that suffering is a normal part of life. And even a casual study of the experience of the saints should persuade us that the serious pursuit of the spiritual life does not eliminate suffering, but may even increase it. The saints did not try to shun adversity, but rather they embraced it as a way of drawing nearer to God. They did not allow a preoccupation with the present blind them to eternal realities. They realized that the cost of giving themselves to God was high, and that trials and troubles were included in the price. The saints set their hearts on perseverance, not on avoidance of hardship. "Best make suffering a good friend," they say, "for it will be your lifelong companion."

In this regard, reflect with me on the life of St. Jane de Chantal, who in my view is a "best practices" example of perseverance in the face of unremitted suffering.

I magine a lovely woman who combined the organizational abilities of an Eleanor Roosevelt, the charismatic charm of an Oprah Winfrey, and the practical spirituality of a Mother Teresa, and you will create a living portrait of St. Jane de Chantal. A marvelous and gifted person, Jane excelled in each of a succession of callings—wife and mother, widow and single parent, and founder and spiritual director of a religious community.

She was madly in love with her soldier-husband, Christophe, Baron de Rabutin-Chantal. For nine years from 1592 to 1601, Madame de Chantal devoted herself to him, administering Bourbilly, his large estate in central France, and raising their four children. Widowed in 1601, for the next nine years Jane committed to remaining single, doubling as mom and dad for her children, managing her staff and farmlands, and all the while exploring ways of opening herself more fully to God. Then, under the guidance of her mentor and friend St. Francis de Sales (1567–1622), she gave her heart more fully to God. And in 1610, in collaboration with Francis, she founded the Sisters of the Visitation of Mary, a community of nuns that divided their time between prayer and serving the poor and the sick.

All of Jane's experience and success in the eighteen years of her first two callings as a wife and widow prepared her for her third as a founder of a religious order. During the three decades before her death in 1641, she established and governed eighty-seven Visitation convents by appointing gifted women to lead them and crisscrossing France in arduous journeys to encourage the nuns in person. Appropriately, Jane became known as Mother de Chantal as she tenderly mothered her sisters as her own daughters. She showered them with affection and personal attention. She corrected them with gentleness, freely forgave their faults, and gave them plenty of space and time to improve at their own pace.

A HUMBLE HEART

Humility is the necessary precondition for being lifted up again by Him, so as to experience the mercy that comes to fill our emptiness. . . . God has a predilection for the humble and, encountering a humble heart, He opens His own fully.

—POPE FRANCIS, General Audience, June 1, 2016

In letters and talks Jane communicated a common-sense approach to daily Christian living that she derived from the teaching of Francis de Sales and her own experience. The hallmarks of her guidance were the innocence, humility, and simplicity that come from giving yourself entirely to God and loving those closest to you with gentleness, forbearance, and service. In my view Jane de Chantal's refreshing idealism and evergreen practicality make her a leading candidate to be recognized as a Doctor of the Church, a designation of respect bestowed only on the very best teachers and exemplars of Christian virtue. She would be a worthy companion to Teresa of Avila (1515–1582), Catherine of Siena (1347–1380), Thérèse of Lisieux (1873–1897), and Hildegard of Bingen (1098–1179), the only other women honored with that title.

St. Jane de Chantal was an extraordinarily successful woman, and our appreciation of her greatness expands exponentially when her achievement is viewed in relief against the trials that dogged her throughout her life. She endured loss, grief, harassment, bad spiritual direction, scruples, doubt, mental anguish, slander, impoverishment, opposition, and more—each serving as a chisel that chipped away her selfish attachments and shaped her in holiness. I admire St. Jane de Chantal for her strengths, but I admire her even more for her weaknesses, from which, with the aid of God's grace, she carved her strengths by sheer perseverance.

A full-length biography would be required to catalog in detail the record of Jane de Chantal's trials and temptations. In this portrait of her endurance I want only to highlight several episodes that show how her spiritual stamina carried her through terrible times. I have chosen to tell about her response to the death of her husband, the persecutions she suffered as a widow, and the doubts and temptations that plagued her after she founded her religious order. I believe that those who face similar trials can find spiritual strength by reflecting on Jane's behavior and imitating the perseverance she showed in these difficult circumstances.

During the nine years of their marriage, Jane bore Christophe six babies, four of whom survived their birth. As a Catholic widower who appreciated the blessing of sexual love, I am thankful for the church's honoring Jane de Chantal as a saintly wife, for she and Christophe had a deep love for each other, and obviously enjoyed its intimate sexual expression.

Christophe served as a warrior in the army of King Henry IV and was often obligated to be at court or in the field. When he was home the chateau at Bourbilly bustled with activity. Jane welcomed many guests and hosted frequent dinners and parties, all the while attending to the children and the business of the estate. But during Christophe's long absences, she withdrew from all social involvements and lived quietly with her little family. In these calmer times, Jane began to sense somewhat vaguely an invitation to a closer relationship to God, which she expressed as prayer for her husband's safety.

In 1601 Christophe left the king's service and came back to stay with his family at Bourbilly. Then one day on a hunting trip his companion's gun accidentally fired and wounded him. Jane, who expected to deliver her fourth child at any moment, personally attended Christophe and begged God to spare him. But after nine days of agony, he died with her at his side.

Christophe's death cleaved Jane's heart. A part of her seemed to die with her beloved husband. She mustered her faith and courageously tried to deal with her extreme grief by busying herself with the care of her four young children and managing her chateau and lands. But her feeling of loss boiled within her. Soon she found it compounded by a swirl of doubts and temptations. "A few months after I became a widow," she later recalled, it pleased God that my whole being should be beset by so many different, distressing temptations that, if he in his mercy had not taken pity on me, I am sure I should have perished in the fury of that storm, for I could get almost no relief from this anxiety, and I lost so much weight that I became quite unlike myself—you would hardly have recognized me.[1]

The temptations that hit Jane while she was mourning would crop up repeatedly throughout her life. She never specified the content of these troubling thoughts, except that she once described them as "suggestions of blasphemy, infidelity, and unbelief."[2] We know only that fear of displeasing God and doubts about faith, probably indistinct and formless, often tormented her. Later St. Francis de Sales would teach her ways of disregarding these temptations, but she was never able to shake them off completely. Now while grieving Christophe's death, the best she could do was to endure them and get through each day, one at a time.

Amid these troubles her growing desire for a closer relationship with God brought Jane some relief, but paradoxically it also contributed to her anxiety. "I was hearing God calling me so clearly," she said,

that had it been possible, I would have left everything and fled into the wilderness, to embrace that vocation in the most thoroughgoing and perfect way, somewhere where I would have been well out of the way of any distractions. I really think that had it not been for the love of my four children obligating me in conscience to remain at home with them, I would have gone, alone and unaided, straight to the Holy Land, to end my days there as an anchoress.[3]

This alternation of doubt and faith that appeared in the early months of Jane's widowhood became the persistent rhythm of her soul. The brightness of God's call would dissipate the darkness of her doubts, but then like nightfall after a beautiful day the darkness would return. I believe that more than anything else the trial of this double-mindedness drew Jane de Chantal near to God and occasioned her holiness.

In 1602 Jane's continuing anguish drove her to seek help from a friar who was giving spiritual direction to several of her acquaintances. This arrogant monk, whose name is unknown and thus unsullied, immediately insisted that she take him as her spiritual director and imposed on her a rigid and oppressive routine of prayer and self-denial. He also required her to vow that she would obey him, never seek direction from another, keep secret everything he told her, and never discuss her spiritual life with anyone but him. Jane had sought spiritual freedom and instead found herself under the control of a small-minded man who imprisoned her soul. Her scrupulosity magnified her pain by compelling her to obey him completely.

In the winter of 1602 another kind of imprisonment tested Jane's endurance. Jane's seventy-five-year-old father-in-law, Guy de Rabutin, a mean-spirited bully, demanded that she come to care for him at Monthelon, his chateau near Autun. If she refused, he threatened to remarry and disinherit her son and three daughters. So Jane steeled herself and moved her little family to his isolated and crowded house, embarking on what one contemporary biographer depicted as "a private purgatory that would last seven years."[4]

Rabutin had taken one of his maids as a mistress and fathered five children by her. The woman, a roughhewn and irascible person, had assumed charge of the chateau. She delighted in telling Jane what to do and peppered her with verbal abuse. Humbly and without complaining about these trials, Jane cared for her father-in-law and the nine children. The persistence of her doubts and the burdensome spiritual regimen imposed on her by her director intensified the stress that she suffered.

Jane spent Lent 1604 in Dijon at the home of her father, Benigné Frémyot. He had invited her to come to hear the daily sermons of that city's famous Lenten preacher, Francis de Sales, the bishop of Geneva. When Jane first saw Francis on Ash Wednesday, she recognized him as the man that God had promised as her spiritual director in a vision several years before. And Francis sensed that she was the woman destined to collaborate with him in founding the innovative community of nuns that was his dream.

SUFFERING TRANSFORMED

By following Jesus, we learn not to knot our lives around problems which become tangled. There will always be problems, always, and when we solve one, another one duly arrives. We can however, find *a new stability*, . . . This stability is called Jesus, who is the Resurrection and the Life. With him, joy abides in our hearts, hope is reborn, suffering is transformed into peace, fear into trust, hardship into an offering of love. And even though burdens will not disappear, there will always be his uplifting hand, his encouraging Word saying to all of us, to each of us: . . . "Come to me!". He tells all of us: "Do not be afraid".

—POPE FRANCIS, Homily, April 2, 2017

For the next six weeks Jane checked her eagerness to pour out her heart to Francis and engaged him only in light conversations. But as Lent progressed her temptations to give up on God escalated to an intolerable level. By Wednesday in Holy Week she felt compelled to seek Francis's counsel. Although she unburdened herself to him with great relief, she did not give him a complete picture of her troubles because of concern to obey her director. In their visits and correspondence over the next several months, Francis gently encouraged Jane to abandon herself to God and pay no attention to her doubts. Finally, late in August he released her from the clutches of the friar and his onerous vows and became her spiritual director. "O Lord, how happy that day was for me!" she said. "I could feel my soul turn completely around and step right out of its inner imprisonment."[5] From that day Jane experienced a greater measure of spiritual freedom and inner peace, but her troubling thoughts were only temporarily quieted.

Francis de Sales regarded Jane de Chantal as ideally gifted to join him in establishing a religious community of women. He appreciated her superior organizational, administrative, and leadership abilities. He esteemed her spiritual strengths even more. Simply devoted to God, brimming with love, eager to serve others, determined to persevere, merciful to a fault, eminently practical in all things—it seemed to Francis that God's invisible hand had picked her as a leader of women and as the cofounder of his order.

LOOK AHEAD
SAINT FRANCES XAVIER CABRINI (1850–1917)

In 1885 St. Frances Xavier Cabrini, founder of the Missionaries of the Sacred Heart, gave the following advice in a letter to one of her sisters:

Why, dearest daughter, do you waste time in sadness when time is so precious for the salvation of poor sinners? Get rid of your melancholy immediately. Don't think any more about yourself. Do not indulge in so many useless and dangerous reflections. Look ahead always without ever looking back. Keep your gaze fixed on the summit of perfection where Christ awaits you.

He wants you despoiled of all things, intent only on procuring his greater glory during this brief time of your existence. For the short time that remains, is it worthwhile to lose yourself in melancholy like those who think only of themselves as if all were to end with this life?

Ah, no. We must not even desire that our pilgrimage on this earth be a short one because we do not yet know the infinite value of every minute employed for the glory of God. Carry your cross then but carry it joyfully, my daughter. Think that Jesus loves you very much. And in return for such love, don't lose yourself in so many desires, but accept daily with serenity whatever comes your way. May the heart of Jesus bless you and make you holy not as you want but as he desires.

—*Letters of Saint Frances Xavier Cabrini*, trans. Ursula Infante (Milan: Ancora, 1970), 24–25.

By 1610 Jane was free to consider opening the first convent of the Sisters of the Visitation of Mary in Annecy. Her eldest daughter had married, her youngest had died, her daughter Françoise was to live with her at the convent, and her only son was entering the court of the French king as a page. Francis, who lived in Annecy, designed the community to accommodate women who were not able or suited for the rigors of the more traditional orders, but who felt called to embrace the religious life. Unlike other communities, the Visitation sisters were not separated from the world in a cloister, did not undertake severe forms of penance and fasting, and were not obliged to pray the Divine Office, the lengthy official prayer of the church. They prayed the shorter Office of Mary and worked to care for their poor and sick neighbors.

Propelled by Jane's charism and inspired by Francis's guidance, within a few years the new order attracted many members and spread quickly to Moulins, Lyons, Paris, and then throughout all France. The road was not easy, for Jane had to deal constantly with poverty, inadequate housing, sickness, internal conflicts, slander, and opposition. When some complained that she was welcoming too many physically ill women into the community, she said, "What am I to do? I happen to like sick people myself."

Jane's hands-on maternal care for her sisters honed her skills as a spiritual teacher and director. Simplicity was the touchstone of her spirituality. She taught the Sisters of the Visitation simply to abandon themselves to God; simply to let the Holy Spirit guide them to pray without worrying about formal methods; simply to accept inconveniences and other involuntary trials and refrain from adopting severe penances; and simply to focus on God and avoid scrutinizing their problems. With her characteristic kindness she helped many women overcome a wide variety of faults and stop being so hard on themselves. But Jane did not extend the same kindness to herself.

Early in their relationship, Francis told Jane that her temptations distressed her because she dreaded them. If she thought less of them, he said, they could not harm her. He summed up his counsel with this memorable example:

Recently I was near the beehives, and some bees flew onto my face. I wanted to raise my hand to brush them off. "No," a peasant said to me. "Don't be afraid and don't touch them. They won't sting you unless you touch them." I trusted him, and not one stung me. Trust me, don't fear these temptations; don't touch them, and they won't hurt you.[6]

Easier said than done. Jane embraced this wisdom and applied it as best she could. But sometimes her doubts swarmed her like bees, and while she did not touch them, their noisy buzzing still tormented her. And they buzzed louder and more menacingly as Jane aged. Through her last nine years Jane felt that she suffered without relief from the same problems she had helped many of her sisters resolve. But she did not falter. Standing firm with the integrity of Job, she simply persevered. In 1641, the year of her death, she affirmed her unflappable decision to endure:

I've had these temptations for forty-one years now—do you think I'm going to give up after all this time? Absolutely not. I'll never stop hoping in God, though he kill me, though he grind me into the dust of eternity (see Job 10:8-9). . . . If I can keep from offending God in spite of all this, then I am content with whatever it may please him to allow me to suffer, even if I must suffer for the rest of my life. I want only to do it knowing that he wants me to, and that in suffering I am being faithful to him.[7]

Unlike the gurus who offer freedom from adversity, the saints make suffering their friend. They embrace hardship as an instrument God uses to shape their character. St. Jane de Chantal's constant trial of doubt and temptation was the chisel that cut away her self-concern and sculpted her spirituality. When hardship struck she did not flinch but received it with a courageous faith. An observation of St. Louis de Montfort (1673–1716), a superb eighteenth-century preacher, accurately describes Jane's endurance and points us down her spiritual path:

> Don't wince under the hammer that strikes you. Have an eye to the chisel that cuts you and to the hand that shapes you. The skillful and loving Architect may wish to make of you the chief stones of his eternal edifice and the fairest statues in his kingdom. Then let him do it. He loves you. He knows what he is doing. He has had experience. All his blows are skillful and straight and loving. He never misses, unless you cause him to by your impatience.[8]

Think, Pray, and Act

Reflecting on the raising of Lazarus from his sepulchre, Pope Francis spoke about our temptations, troubles and hardships:

> "Each one of us already has a small sepulchre, some area that has somewhat died within our hearts; a wound, a wrongdoing endured or inflicted, an unrelenting resentment, a regret that keeps coming back, a sin we cannot overcome. Today, let us identify these little sepulchres that we have inside, and let us invite Jesus *into them.*"[9]

Use the following questions to identify your trials, challenges, and problems and to seek the Lord's way to overcome them or persevere through them.

Think

🏃 Ask the following questions in order to take stock of your life circumstances. What trials am I experiencing? Loss? Addiction? Illness? Family concerns? Relationship problems? Other?

🏃 What have I done to eliminate the cause, solve the problem, or deal with the issue that produces each trial? Pray? Reflect on Scripture? Go to confession? Get counseling or medical help? Other?

🏃 What else might I do to deal with the source of the trial?

Pray

🏃   Take a quiet half hour to pray about your trials. Read Romans 8:18–39. Notice that the Holy Spirit prays for you (verse 26) and that Jesus intercedes for you (verse 34).

🏃   Ask the Lord to help you deal with the root cause of the trial.

🏃   Ask the Lord to give you the grace to persevere in trials that he allows to continue in your life.

Act

🏃   Decide what possible steps you could take to resolve the matter behind the trials in your life.

🏃   For persistent trials, imitate the perseverance of St. Jane de Chantal. For daily strength and support, read and meditate on Romans 8:26–39.

May you always find the wisdom to discover the root causes of your trials. May you grab on to the grace Jesus offers to set you free and stabilize your life. And may you embrace his advice: "Do not be afraid!" Ever.

Ten JOY
BLESSED PIER GIORGIO FRASSATI (1901–1925)

How blessed are the poor in spirit; the kingdom of Heaven is theirs.
—*Matthew 5:3*

Be merry, really merry. The life of a true Christian should be a perpetual jubilee, a prelude to the festivals of eternity.
—*St. Théophane Vénard (1829–1861)*

"The Christian identity card is joy, . . . the joy of having been chosen by Jesus, saved by Jesus, regenerated by Jesus; the Christian knows that God remembers him, that God loves him, that God accompanies him, that God is waiting for him. And this is joy.
—POPE FRANCIS, Homily, May 23, 2016

Pier Giorgio Frassati has become the hero of contemporary young Catholics, because they see themselves in him. They recognize that he held himself to a high Christian ideal, while pursuing the same pleasures that they enjoy. They gravitate to this handsome and charming saint who organized mountain-climbing expeditions and parties for his friends—and who, at the same time, delighted in reciting the poetry of Dante, praying the Rosary in his booming voice, and spending a night in adoration of the Blessed Sacrament.

Pope John Paul II and Pier Giorgio's biographers celebrate him as a man of the Beatitudes. That he was poor in spirit and pure of heart was obvious to all, but he manifested these divine qualities in a very balanced and human way. Athletic and strong, he devoted himself to the weak and malformed. He was wealthy, but he lived in poverty so he could give everything to the poor. He was gregarious, but a lover of solitude. He was rambunctious, the life of every party, and a practical joker, but at prayer he was solemn, reflective, and quiet.

One of my favorite photographs of Pier Giorgio shows him descending an Alpine mountain, smiling with a pipe in his mouth. He used to quip that he liked smoking because his mother had smoked cigars when she nursed him.[1] Another of my favorites has him and several buddies cheerfully dragging a barrel of wine to some festivity.[2] But I also carry in my memory the testimony of his friend who reported that when Pier Giorgio left a church after an hour of prayer, he would turn and give a little wave toward the tabernacle. I regard that affectionate gesture as emblematic of his closeness to Jesus.

Catholic young people today love Pier Giorgio because, unlike other saints who appear to them to be otherworldly, they regard him as "normal"—showing them that they can live the Christian life in our thoroughly secularized world. They freely imitate his piety that centered on the Eucharist, Scripture, and Mary. His selfless care for the poor challenges them to dedicate themselves to Christian service. One biographer called Pier Giorgio an "ordinary" Christian, but if so, being an ordinary Christian means putting God first in everything and spending yourself entirely for others.

In this concluding chapter, I present Pier Giorgio Frassati as a portrait of the normal Christian life. I have titled it "Joy" because he bore great sorrows joyfully beneath the enthusiastic surface of his service, friendships, politics, sport, and fun. His happiness did not depend upon externals. Rather his joy stemmed from an intimate relationship with Jesus, which enabled him to be happy in the midst of painful circumstances, especially in his difficult relationship with his parents. "My life is monotonous," he once said, "but each day I understand a little better the incomparable grace of being a Catholic. Down, then, with all melancholy. That should never find a place except in the heart which has lost faith. I am joyful. Sorrow is not gloom. Gloom should be banished from the Christian soul."[3]

Pier Giorgio Frassati was born in Turin, Italy, on April 6, 1901. His sister, Luciana, who became his closest friend, was born seventeen months later. His father, Alfredo Frassati, owned and edited *La Stampa,* an influential liberal newspaper. Adelaide Ametis, his mother, was an artist whose wealthy family owned a villa at Pollone, fifty miles from the Frassati home in Turin.

From childhood, Pier Giorgio experienced a tension-filled family life because his parents had drifted apart. Their frequent arguments made for an acidic household environment. Adelaide and the children summered at Pollone while Alfredo stayed in Turin to manage his newspaper. This annual separation symbolized the deterioration of their marriage. The alienation of his parents from each other, which only intensified over the years, saddened Pier Giorgio with a heartache that he felt daily.

The family situation toughened Pier Giorgio's character and subtly drew him to Christ, but his parents did little to encourage his spiritual formation. He received his religious training from priests and nuns at school. Alfredo was an agnostic and was displeased with Pier Giorgio's spirituality. Once he complained to a priest that he found his preteen son asleep on the floor with a rosary in his hand. The priest, who had baptized Pier Giorgio, caught Alfredo up short with his reply: "Perhaps you would rather have him fall asleep with a dirty novel?"[4]

Adelaide did not like or understand Pier Giorgio's religious inclinations, which she worried might lead him to the priesthood instead of a secular career.[5] When a Jesuit invited her twelve-year-old son to daily Mass and Communion, she strenuously opposed the idea. She feared that it would make him a narrow-minded Catholic. But after several days of Pier Giorgio's begging, she relented.[6] And from that time daily Mass and Communion became his routine.

HOLINESS FOR ALL
Saint Francis de Sales (1567–1622)

In his Introduction to the Devout Life, *St. Francis de Sales showed how ordinary people, who are locked daily into worldly routines, could live saintly lives. He addressed his reader as Philothea, a soul who loves God:*

Very often, under color of an alleged impossibility, people who are obliged to live an ordinary life are not willing even to think of undertaking the devout life. . . . They are of the opinion that, just as no animal dare taste of the herb called *palma Christi* [castor oil plant], so no one ought to aspire to the palm of Christian piety, while living in the midst of the press of worldly occupations. And I show them that as the mother-of-pearl fish live in the sea without taking in one drop of salt water, . . . so a vigorous and constant soul can live in the world without receiving any worldly taint. . . .

No, Philothea, true devotion does us no harm whatsoever, but instead perfects all things. When it goes contrary to a man's lawful vocation, it is undoubtedly false. "The bee," Aristotle says, "extracts honey out of flowers without hurting them" and leaves them as whole and fresh as it finds them. True devotion does better still. It not only does no injury to one's vocation, but on the contrary adorns and beautifies it. All kinds of precious stones take on greater luster when dipped into honey, each according to its color. So also every vocation becomes more agreeable when united with devotion. Care of one's family is rendered more peaceable, love of husband and wife more sincere, service of one's prince more faithful, and every type of employment more pleasant and agreeable.

—Adapted from St. Francis de Sales, *Introduction to the Devout Life,* trans. John K. Ryan (New York: Image Books, 1989), 33, 44.

When Pier Giorgio and Luciana reached their teen years, the family's relationships deteriorated even further. Neither Pier Giorgio nor his sister were very good students, and both Adelaide and Alfredo expressed displeasure at their academic failures. Alfredo sometimes called Pier Giorgio stupid, hoping to spur him to success, but it only pushed him away. Family tensions erupted at mealtimes, with Alfredo and Adelaide arguing vigorously and Pier Giorgio and Luciana withdrawing into silence. Pier Giorgio dreaded suppertime and often came late. Luciana says he made the sign of the cross before entering the dining room. And in response to his tardiness, Adelaide would comment, "There he is lost in his thoughts. He remembers Mass times but not meal times."[7]

In 1918, at the age of seventeen, Pier Giorgio joined the St. Vincent de Paul Society. As he began to visit poor people, he fell in love with them. Turin teemed with jobless veterans who had returned from World War I. Destitute laboring families had also poured into the city, attracted to its growing industries. Delivering food, clothing, and money to these needy people became Pier Giorgio's daily passion. His works of mercy took precedence over both school and family. In a typical week, his acts of kindness looked something like this: Sunday, galoshes for a barefoot child; Monday, a room for a homeless woman; Tuesday, boots for an unemployed laborer; Thursday, relocation for a blind veteran; Friday, groceries for a hungry family; Saturday, medicine for an old man with bronchitis.[8] Adelaide did not realize that this selfless giving, not some scatterbrained religiosity, accounted for her son's recurrent lateness to dinner. Frequently, he had to run home from the slums because he had given a beggar his money for the train.

Pier Giorgio impoverished himself in order to give as much as he could to the poor. When a friend asked why he traveled uncomfortably on trains in third class, he said, "Because there's not a fourth class." That response symbolized his selflessness. Once in twelve-degree-below-zero weather, Pier Giorgio came home wearing a smile but no overcoat, which he had given to an elderly homeless man. Alfredo angrily confronted him, but he disarmed his father by simply saying, "But you see, Dad, it was cold."[9] As a graduation present Alfredo gave him the choice of a car or its value in cash. He took the money and invested it in the people who needed it more. Luciana shared a thousand lire from her wedding gifts with her brother on the condition that he would use it for himself. But Pier Giorgio gave five hundred lire to the St. Vincent de Paul society for furniture. He anonymously donated the remaining five hundred lire to help a disabled man set up a sherbet stand to support his family.[10]

EMBRACING THE POOR

I want a Church which is poor and for the poor. They have much to teach us. Not only do they share in the sensus fidei, but in their difficulties they know the suffering Christ. We need to let ourselves be evangelized by them. The new evangelization is an invitation to acknowledge the saving power at work in their lives and to put them at the centre of the Church's pilgrim way. We are called to find Christ in them, to lend our voice to their causes, but also to be their friends, to listen to them, to speak for them and to embrace the mysterious wisdom which God wishes to share with us through them.

—POPE FRANCIS, *The Joy of the Gospel,* 198

Pier Giorgio especially enjoyed his relationships with those he served. For example, one day a shopkeeper volunteered to distribute his gifts for him, but he declined. "I prefer to deliver the packages personally, because that way I can also encourage the people a bit, give them hope that their lives will change, and above all I can convince them to offer their sufferings to God and to go to Mass."[11]

A friend once asked Pier Giorgio why the filth of the hovels he visited did not repulse him. "Jesus comes to me every morning in Holy Communion," he replied. "I repay him in my very small way by visiting the poor. The house may be sordid, but I am going to Christ."[12] With these few words Pier Giorgio revealed the heart of his spirituality. The joy that dissipated the sorrows of his life flowed from his intimacy with Jesus. He expressed his love for Christ in his service to the poor. He sustained it with a sacramental, scriptural, and Marian piety.

Pier Giorgio loved Jesus in the Eucharist. He rose early every morning to worship him at Mass and receive him in Communion before the day began. He even scheduled his excursions to the mountains to ensure his attendance at Mass, no matter how inconvenient. He spent many hours each week in local churches, silently adoring the Lord in the Blessed Sacrament. "After a prayer vigil," he said, "I feel stronger, safer, more secure, and even happier." Once, according to a friend, he became so absorbed in prayer during an all-night vigil that he did not notice wax from a large candle dripping on his head.[13] Pier Giorgio also drew spiritual strength by frequenting the sacrament of Reconciliation. On one memorable occasion he bumped into a priest friend on the road and asked him to hear his confession. The priest pointed to a nearby church where they could go, but Pier Giorgio uninhibitedly made his confession on the street.[14]

Pier Giorgio grounded his spirituality on Scripture, especially the letters of St. Paul, which he also urged his friends to read. As a reminder of the motive for his acts of kindness, he posted a copy of

1 Corinthians 13—Paul's magnificent hymn to love—on his desk. He regularly read *The Imitation of Christ,* which, along with the New Testament, he included in his gift packages to poor families. He relieved the boredom of his studies by reading St. Augustine's *Confessions.* "Never before," he wrote to a friend, "have I found such endless enjoyment, because in reading Augustine's powerful *Confessions,* we get a glimpse of the joy reserved for those who die under the sign of the cross."[15]

Pier Giorgio complemented his love for Christ in the sacraments and Scripture with a lively devotion to Mary. He always had a rosary at hand and prayed it several times a day, often inviting his friends to join him. He tacked on his bedroom door St. Bernard's prayer to the Virgin from Dante's *Paradiso:* "Lady, you are so great and accessible, that anyone who wants grace and fails to ask your intercession—his desire tries to fly without wings."[16] When he was at Pollone he made daily pilgrimages to the shrine of the Madonna of Oropa, about five miles from the villa. In order to wake up before the family, he designed a unique alarm. He tied a rope around his foot and dropped it out the window, so that the gardener could pull it and awaken him.[17] At the shrine he asked Mary to intercede for his family and friends. One time he requested her protection for a friend who was training to be a pilot: "On the twenty-seventh I will be hiking up to Oropa," he wrote his friend in a letter that captures the spirit of Pier Giorgio's Marian piety,

> and I will pray for you at the feet of the Black Madonna, for whatever my prayers are worth. As soon as I get back to Turin, I will send you a keepsake: a rosary made from the seeds of some garden plant, to which I will attach a medal of the Madonna of Loreto. May the Virgin Mary watch over you when you "ride with the wind" (See Psalm 104:3).[18]

In May 1922 Pier Giorgio joined the Third Order of St. Dominic, a serious step in preparation for his vocation of service to the poor. As a tertiary, he took the name Girolamo, after Girolamo Savonarola, the fifteenth-century Dominican. He thought highly of the controversial Savonarola, who had championed social and political reform in the city of Florence and had opposed its corrupt de Medici rulers. He told a friend he wanted to imitate his namesake: "I am a fervent admirer of this friar, who died as a saint at the stake. In becoming a tertiary I wanted to take him as a model, but I am far from being like him."[19] (Although Savonarola had been excommunicated and executed because of his attacks on the Roman Curia and the pope, some Dominicans in Pier Giorgio's day believed that he had been unfairly treated and formed a movement to have Savonarola canonized.)

Pier Giorgio's fascination with Savonarola indicates that he intended to spend his life working for social change. Although Pier Giorgio found joy in his personal service to the poor, he also wanted to help relieve the causes of poverty. As a university student, he decided to major in mechanical engineering at Turin's Royal Polytechnic so that he could work with miners, who were considered the lowest of the working classes, and contribute to improving their life circumstances.[20]

Impressed with the activism of the German priest Fr. Karl Sonneshein and the Italian priest Fr. Luigi Sturzo, Pier Giorgio considered working for societal reform as a priest. But ultimately he made a strategic decision to pursue his goals as a layman. In the fall of 1921, Pier Giorgio visited Freiburg, Germany, where he stayed with the Rahner family, whose two sons, Karl and Hugo, would later become Jesuits. Their mother, Louise Rahner, remembered that Pier Giorgio told her he had decided not to become a priest because he could do more for the poor as a layman. "I want to do whatever I can to help my people," he had said,

> and I think I can do this better as a layman than as a priest, because at home priests are not in such close contact with the people as they are here in Germany. By giving good example as a mining engineer, I can actually be much more effective.[21]

Pier Giorgio translated his idealism into action. He participated as a leader in student political organizations and joined Luigi Sturzo's Popular Party. He had a vision of uniting professionals with workers in order to form a body of leaders who could collaborate to improve conditions for Italy's lower classes. He proposed such a union of forces to a political congress at Ravenna in 1921. Although his initiative was defeated, it demonstrated that in addition to his personal acts of charity, he was working for structural changes in society to help the poor.[22]

The rise of Mussolini and Fascism in the early 1920s distressed Pier Giorgio, and he courageously resisted the movement. At great personal risk, he worked with opposition parties and marched in anti-Fascist demonstrations. He spoke openly against Mussolini and his party, denouncing them publicly. At least the Communists had the ideal of raising the working class, he said. "But what ideals do the Fascists have? Filthy lucre, paid by the industrialists and, shamefully, by our government."[23] Pier Giorgio could hardly control his rage when Mussolini came to power in October 1922 with the limited support of the Popular Party. "I glanced at Mussolini's speech," he wrote,

> and my blood boiled. I am disappointed by the really shameful behavior of the Popular Party. Where is the fine

program, where is the faith which motivates our people? But when it is a matter of turning out for worldly honors, people trample on their own conscience.[24]

For Pier Giorgio, involvement in politics and social reform was an act of faith. And his sacramental piety fired his fervor. Every morning when the priest concluded Mass, saying, "*Ite, missa est!*" ("Go, you are sent!"), he accepted it as the Lord's charge to work for justice in his world. For him, observed Luciana, "living in society meant struggling for the Spirit to return, reactivating it where it was feeble and kindling it where it did not exist."[25]

Lighthearted fun with friends occupied much of the last year of Pier Giorgio's short life. He and his closest comrades had organized themselves into "The Shady Character's Society," a merry group of young men and women that indulged in good times. Each member had an office, and Pier Giorgio was designated "practical joker," a role that he already played very well. He and a friend constituted "The Terror" subsection of the club. They cracked jokes, played hoaxes, short-sheeted beds, and once sent a little donkey to a member who hated studying.[26] I can imagine what they might have done with duct tape, had it been invented. The society gathered for mountain-climbing expeditions, which Pier Giorgio planned and directed. At mountain tops he led his friends in prayer, celebrating the One who created the majestic peaks. After the climb, they relaxed and enjoyed food, wine, cigars, and songs. On these joyful occasions Pier Giorgio sang loudly in his deep voice. He knew he was always off-key, but protested that "the important thing is to sing."[27]

JOY ENDURES TRIALS

Joy is not expressed the same way at all times in life, especially at moments of great difficulty. Joy adapts and changes, but it always endures, even as a flicker of light born of our personal certainty that, when everything is said and done, we are infinitely loved. I understand the grief of people who have to endure great suffering, yet slowly but surely we all have to let the joy of faith slowly revive as a quiet yet firm trust, even amid the greatest distress.

—POPE FRANCIS, *The Joy of the Gospel*, 6

However, this year of fun with friends masked deep sorrows that roiled in Pier Giorgio's heart. He had fallen in love with Laura Hidalgo, one of the young women in the group. He kept his feelings for her secret, never telling her or anyone except Luciana about them. His heart's desire was to marry her, but he knew that his father and mother would not approve of her as an appropriate wife for him because they wanted their son to marry someone of higher social status. Alfredo and Adelaide were on the verge of officially separating. Pier Giorgio believed that a decision to marry Laura would cause his parents to end their marriage. He could not bring himself to destroy one family by starting another. So he quietly bore the pain of saying no to his unspoken love.[28]

Then in 1925, when Pier Giorgio was about to graduate and begin working with miners to improve their lot, Alfredo sabotaged his dream. He decided that Pier Giorgio should be trained to become the manager of *La Stampa*. Reluctant to break the news himself, he had a business associate tell his decision to his son. Although dumbfounded and profoundly disappointed, Pier Giorgio acquiesced. "Do you think this will please my Dad?" he asked the messenger, who nodded yes. "Then tell him I accept."[29]

But the Lord claimed Pier Giorgio in death before this could happen. During the last days of June 1925, he became very ill. No one in the Frassati household paid much attention to him, as all were preoccupied with his grandmother, who also was dying. They thought his sickness would pass quickly, but polio, which he had probably caught from one of his beloved poor, aggressively ravished his body. He was unable to attend his grandmother's funeral, and Adelaide ironically complained that he was never available when he was needed. When the family finally realized the seriousness of his illness, it was too late. Even on his deathbed, his love for the poor was first in Pier Giorgio's thoughts. He asked Luciana to deliver some medicine to a sick man and to renew an insurance policy for a poor man on his behalf.[30] He died on July 4, 1925.

The sudden death of the beloved young man left everyone in shock. Thousands of Turin's poor came to the funeral to honor their benefactor, and their numbers astounded Alfredo and Adelaide as they finally realized the extent of their son's generosity and service. Pier Giorgio's friends suffered boundless grief. Two days after his death, one of the young women whom Pier Giorgio had served wrote to Marco Beltramo, his close friend. In her letter, Clementina Luotti expressed the grievous loss that they all felt:

> Now I recognize that I was so unworthy to be near that soul; and the thought makes me tremble. . . . I cannot pray—I do not say for him, which would sound like madness—that he may help me to deserve to remember him. I think that— as punishment to me—the Gospel threat has come true: "I will strike the shepherd and the sheep will be scattered" (see Mark 14:27). It was his goodness that kept us united. . . . Oh, the marvelous youthfulness that emanated from him and floated around him, which made us so light-hearted, ready

to take a plunge, so free of any mortal hindrance, so close to God who was in him! Who will ever give us this purifying joy again? Who will renew not only under our eyes but in us the miracle of joyful holiness, carefree and fresh and reviving as water from an Alpine spring?[31]

I am thankful that Clementina was ultimately wrong. Pier Giorgio Frassati was beatified by Pope John Paul II on May 20, 1990. Now as a saint, he renews in many of us who love him the miracle of joyful holiness.

With Pope Francis let's celebrate Pier Giorgio with this blessing: May the Lord give us joy, the joy of our lives and of having our hearts at peace even when faced with many difficulties. And may he protect us from seeking happiness in so many things that ultimately sadden us: they promise much, but they will not give us anything! Remember well: a Christian is a man, and a woman, of joy, joy in the Lord; a man and a woman of wonder ."[32]

Think, Pray, and Act

Take stock of your life. Are you pursuing holiness in the ordinary circumstances of your life? Are you living joyfully?

Think

Using Pier Giorgio's life as a measure for comparison, ask yourself how well you are doing in key areas of normal Christian living:

- What means do I use to express my love for God? How faithful am I in expressing my love for God?

- In what ways do I express my love for others? How faithful am I in expressing my love for others?

Ө   Am I experiencing joy in my daily circumstances? Why or why not?

Pray

Ө   Take half an hour of quiet time to pray and ask the Holy Spirit what *one* thing you could do to live the normal Christian life more effectively.

Ө   What might be *one* change you could make that would help you become more joyful?

Act

Ө   Once you have determined what you can do to live the normal Christian life more effectively, develop a simple plan to implement your decision. Figure out the easiest way to make it happen. Then do it for a predetermined period of time. At the end of the period, review how well you have done. Consider renewing or revising your plan.

May you live a normal Christian life of love and joy. And by God's grace may you conduct your ordinary life in extraordinary ways.

Afterword
NO EXCUSES

There is but one sadness—not to be a saint.
—*French novelist Léon Blois*

We all take a different road, but each one leads to the same goal. You and I must have a single aim—to grow in holiness while following the way God in his goodness has laid down for us.
—*St. Thérèse of Lisieux*

Do not be afraid of holiness. It will take away none of your energy, vitality or joy. On the contrary, you will become what the Father had in mind when he created you, and you will be faithful to your deepest self.
—POPE FRANCIS, *Rejoice and Be Glad*, 32

Recently, I imagined that three readers of *Saints at Heart* appeared to me in a dream. They came to thank me for the book, which they liked very much. But they wanted to explain why they could not become saints. They all spoke as if there were an asterisk on God's call to holiness that meant that they were excused from it.

The first visitor was a single mother of two small children, a toddler and a baby, who sat on her lap and constantly interrupted her as she spoke. She believed that becoming a saint seemed too difficult for her. With all of the challenges she faced as a single parent, she wondered how she could imitate saints who spent hours praying, serving the poor, and spreading the gospel. I told her that she was making the pursuit of holiness too hard for herself. She didn't need to walk around barefoot preaching the gospel, or go off to a foreign land to evangelize non-Christians, or found a community to care for marginalized people. She just needed to decide to be a saint and then do with love the things she had to do as a single mother. I assured her that she could be a saint who nursed a baby, helped a toddler learn the alphabet, washed the dishes, went to her job, and collapsed in exhaustion at the end of the day.

My second visitor was a young man, about thirty years old, who had never been able to get his life on track. He had dropped out of college and worked now as a clerk at a video store. He spent his nights hanging out with his friends. He came to explain that he was just too rotten to become a saint. He didn't go into great detail, but he said that he was guilty of some serious wrongdoing, had some bad habits, and was addicted to alcohol. So I told him stories about saints who had been big sinners. I spoke about St. Peter, who had denied Jesus; St. Camillus de Lellis (1550–1614), who was a gambling addict; Matt Talbot (1856–1925), who was an alcoholic; and St. Augustine (354–430), who struggled with chastity. I also suggested that he reread the chapter in my book about Dorothy Day, a saint who had been an atheist and a prodigal. Then I invited him to make a fresh start. I urged him to turn to Jesus, who loved him just as he was; to turn away from his sins; and to decide to pursue holiness. His sinfulness, I said, was no excuse for not becoming a saint—it was an opportunity.

The last guest in my dream was a sixty-six-year-old grandmother. She came to say that while she found holiness attractive, it was just too late for her to decide to become a saint. She felt that her pattern of life was set in stone—visiting grandkids, reading her novels, and watching *Jeopardy* and her other favorite TV programs. When she finished her litany of reasons why she was too old to get started on sanctity, I told her about saints who were late bloomers. We talked, for example, about St. Teresa of Avila (1515–1582), who said that for twenty years she had been a gadabout nun. She was forty years old before she responded to grace and began to pursue holiness aggressively. So I helped my visitor see that her age was not an excuse for not deciding to become a saint.

You didn't make an appearance in my dream, so I hope you are not tempted to make excuses why you can't decide to become a saint. There really are no excuses, only missed opportunities.

A few years ago, the elderly father of my friend George Martin died three weeks after he fell and broke his shoulder and pelvis. Arthur Martin was a clear-thinking, ninety-eight-year-old retired chemist who still personally managed his investments. On his first day at a rehabilitation center, a social worker had asked him a battery of questions. Her final question was, "What is your goal now?" She expected him to say something like, "To recover and be able to take care of myself again." But after a moment of reflection, he said, "To live a holy life."

What is your goal now?

Notes

Foreword (pp. 9–13)

1 *The Story of a Soul*, 3rd ed., trans. John Clarke (Washington, DC: ICS Publications, 1996), 28.

2 *The Story of a Soul*, 175.

3 *Thomas Merton, Spiritual Master: The Essential Writings* (Ossining, NY: Orbis, 2000), 377.

4 Thomas Merton, *The Seven Storey Mountain* (New York: Mariner Books, 1999), 41.

5 All Saints Day, homily, 2nd Reading.

6 Abbé François Trochu, *Bernadette Soubirous, 1844–1879* (Rockford, IL: Tan Books, 1987), 310.

7 *The Rule of St. Benedict*, Prologue, verse 46.

Introduction (pp. 15–17)

1 Pope Francis, *Rejoice and Be Glad, 1*.

2 Pope Benedict XVI, General Audience, January 31, 2007, reported in *The Florida Catholic*, February 9–15, 2007, A9.

3 Pope John Paul II, Message for the Annual World Day of Prayer for Vocations (*I discepoli*; November 1, 1991), in *The Pope Speaks* (vol. 37, no. 3; May/June 1992), 131.

ONE Loving God: Saint Thérèse of Lisieux (pp. 19–32)

1 John Beevers, *Saint Thérèse, the Little Flower: The Making of a Saint* (Rockford, IL: Tan Books, 1976), 124.

2 *Butler's Lives of the Saints: New Full Edition*, ed. David Hugh Farmer (Collegeville, MN: The Liturgical Press, 1996), October, 3.

3 *The Autobiography of Saint Thérèse of Lisieux: The Story of a Soul*, trans. John Beevers (New York: Doubleday Image Books, 1989).

4 Beevers, *Autobiography,* 130.

5 Joseph E. Schmidt, *Praying with Thérèse of Lisieux* (Frederick, MD: The Word Among Us Press, 1991), 17.

6 Beevers, *Autobiography,* 26.

7 Beevers, *Autobiography,* 53.

8 Beevers, *Autobiography,* 46.

9 Beevers, *Autobiography,* 61.

10 Beevers, *Autobiography,* 62–63.

11 Beevers, *Autobiography,* 74.

12 Beevers, *Autobiography,* 84.

13 Beevers, *Autobiography,* 85.

14 Beevers, *Autobiography,* 109.

15 Beevers, *Autobiography,* 110.

16 *Butler's Lives of the Saints,* October, 2.

17 Beevers, *Autobiography,* 100.

18 Beevers, *Autobiography,* 99.

19 Beevers, *Autobiography,* 108.

20 Beevers, *Autobiography,* 138.

21 Beevers, *Autobiography,* 136.

22 Beevers, *Autobiography,* 113–14.

23 Beevers, *Autobiography,* 122.

24 Beevers, *Autobiography,* 156.

TWO Loving Others: Saint Aelred of Rievaulx (pp. 33–43)

1 Douglass Roby, introduction to Aelred of Rievaulx, *Spiritual Friendship*, trans. Mary Eugenia Laker, Cistercian Fathers Series 5 (Kalmazoo, MI: Cistercian Publications, 1977), 7.

2 The Cistercian Order was named for the mother house at Cîteaux, which had been founded in 1098 by several monks who sought to establish a community following a strict observance of monastic discipline. Bernard's community at Clairvaux was also a Cistercian monastery.

3 Walter Daniel, *The Life of Ailred of Rievaulx*, trans. F. M. Powicke (London: Thomas Nelson and Sons, 1950), 25.

4 F. M. Powicke, in introduction to Daniel, *The Life of Ailred of Rievaulx*, lvii and lviii.

5 Charles Dumont, in introduction to Aelred Rievaulx, *The Mirror of Charity*, trans. Elizabeth Connor (Kalamazoo, MI: Cistercian Publications, 1990), 50–51.

6 Roby, *Spiritual Friendship*, 19–20.

7 "Pastoral Prayer," adapted from James Brodrick, *A Procession of Saints* (New York: Longmans, Green and Co., 1949), 10.

8 Daniel, *The Life of Ailred of Rievaulx*, 40.

9 *Butler's Lives of the Saints*, January, 82.

10 Daniel, *The Life of Ailred of Rievaulx*, 79.

11 Daniel, *The Life of Ailred of Rievaulx*, 40.

12 Roby, *Spiritual Friendship*, 23.

13 Cf. 1 John 4:16; Daniel, *Spiritual Friendship* 1.70, 66.

14 Cited in Aelred Squire, *Aelred of Rievaulx: A Study* (London: SPCK, 1963), 49–50, 111.

THREE Conversion: Saint Francis of Assisi (pp. 44–55)

1 Thomas of Celano, *First Life of St. Francis*, in *Writings and Early Biographies: English Omnibus of the Sources for the Life of St. Francis*, ed. Marion E. Habig (Chicago: Franciscan Herald Press, 1983), 230.

2 Thomas of Celano, *Second Life of St. Francis*, in *Writings and Early Biographies*, 363.

3 Thomas of Celano, *Second Life*, 364.

4 Thomas of Celano, *First Life*, 232.

5 Thomas of Celano, *Second Life*, 365.

6 Thomas of Celano, *Second Life*, 366.

7 Johannes Jörgensen, *St. Francis of Assisi: A Biography* (Garden City, NJ: Image Books, 1955), 32.

8 Jörgensen, *St. Francis of Assisi*, 32.

9 Based on Jörgensen, p. 38, and *Second Life*, p. 369.

10 Adapted from *The Testament of St. Francis*, in *Writings and Early Biographies*, 67.

11 Thomas of Celano, *Second Life*, 370.

12 Thomas of Celano, *Second Life*, 371.

13 Omer Englebert, *St. Francis of Assisi: A Biography* (Ann Arbor, MI: Servant, 1979), 36.

14 Adapted from Thomas of Celano, *Second Life*, 372, and Englebert, *St. Francis of Assisi: A Biography*, 36.

15 Thomas of Celano, *First Life*, 247.

FOUR Calling: Saint Katharine Drexel (pp. 56–66)

1 Pope Francis, Message for the 2018 World Day of Vocations, December 3, 2017.

2 In Mary van Balen Holt, *Meet Katharine Drexel* (Ann Arbor, MI: Servant Publications, 2002), 16.

3 In Holt, *Meet Katharine Drexel*, 25.

4 See Acts 9:36.

5 Holt, *Meet Katharine Drexel*, 26.

6 In Holt, *Meet Katharine Drexel*, 28.

7 In Consuela Marie Duffy, *Katharine Drexel: A Biography* (Bethlehem, PA: Mother Katharine Drexel Guild, 1987), 60–61.

8 Duffy, *Katharine Drexel: A Biography,* 113–15.

9 Holt, *Meet Katharine Drexel,* 40.

10 Duffy, *Katharine Drexel,* 100.

11 Holt, *Meet Katharine Drexel,* Holt, 58–59.

12 Holt, *Meet Katharine Drexel,* 60–63.

13 Holt, *Meet Katharine Drexel,* 64.

FIVE Prayer and Study: Dorothy Day (pp. 67–85)

1 Pope Francis, *Rejoice and Be Glad,* 107.

2 *The Catholic Worker* (February 1940), cited in Mary and Louise "Dorothy Day and the Catholic Worker Movement" in Dorothy Day, *On Pilgrimage,* 1–64 (Grand Rapids, MI: Wm. B. Eerdmans, 1999), Zwick, 18.

3 Dorothy Day, *Union Square to Rome,* chapter 2, in Dorothy Day Library, http:// www .catholicworker.org/dorothyday/daytext.cfm?TextID=202&SearchTerm=bible (consulted December 21, 2006).

4 Day, *Union Square to Rome,* chapter 2.

5 Dorothy Day, *The Long Loneliness* (Garden City, NJ: Image Books, 1959), 26–27. The Benedicite is the prayer of the three young men in the fiery furnace; see Daniel 3.

6 Brigid O'Shea Merriman, *Searching for Christ: The Spirituality of Dorothy Day* (Notre Dame, IN: University of Notre Dame Press, 1994), 7.

7 Day, *Long Loneliness,* 36.

8 Day, *Long Loneliness,* 37–38.

9 Day, *Long Loneliness,* 39–41.

10 Merriman, *Searching for Christ,* 11.

11 Day, *Long Loneliness,* 78.

12 Day, *Long Loneliness,* 78.

13 Day, *Long Loneliness,* 82.

14 Merriman, *Searching for Christ,* 15–16.

15 Day, *Long Loneliness,* 104.

16 Day, *Long Loneliness,* 105.

17 Day, *Long Loneliness,* 130.

18 Day, *Long Loneliness,* 112.

19 Day, *Long Loneliness,* 145.

20 Day, *Long Loneliness,* 145; Romano Guardini (1885–1968) was a Roman Catholic priest, author, and academic who taught at the Universities of Berlin, Tübingen, and Munich.

21 Day, *Long Loneliness,* 161; Merriman, *Searching for Christ: The Spirituality of Dorothy Day,* 22–23.

22 James Allaire and Rosemary Broughton, *Praying with Dorothy Day* (Winona, MN: Saint Mary's Press, 1995), 21.

23 Day, *Long Loneliness,* 166.

24 Day, *Long Loneliness,* 169.

25 Dorothy Day, "Liturgy and Sociology," *The Catholic Worker* (January 1936), 5, in Dorothy Day Library, http://www.catholicworker.org/dorothyday/daytext .cfm?TextID=202&SearchTerm=bible (consulted December 21, 2006).

26 *Day,* "Liturgy and Sociology," 5.

27 In Merriman, *Searching for Christ,* 8.

28 *The Catholic Worker* (July–August 1973), in Dorothy Day Library, http://www .catholicworker.org/dorothyday/daytext.cfm?TextID=202&SearchTerm=bible (consulted December 21, 2006).

29 *The Catholic Worker* (July–August 1973).

30 Jean Walsh, in Rosalie G. Riegle, *Dorothy Day: Portraits by Those Who Knew Her* (Maryknoll, NY: Orbis Books, 2003), 80.

31 Jim Forest, in Riegle, *Dorothy Day*, 80.

32 Dorothy Gauchat, in Riegle, *Dorothy Day*, 82.

SIX Community: Saint Angela Merici (pp. 86–97)

1 Jn 17:21; Pope Francis, *Rejoice and Be Glad*, 146.

2 *Butler's Lives of the Saints*, 186. Although St. Ursula was a popular saint in the Middle Ages, Pope Paul VI removed her from the calendar of saints and suppressed her feast in 1969 because she is suspected to be a legendary figure.

3 Philip Caraman, *Saint Angela: The Life of Angela Merici Foundress of the Ursulines* (New York: Farrar, Straus and Company, 1963), 15–16; Omer Englebert, *St. Francis of Assisi: A Biography* (Ann Arbor, MI: Servant Publications, 1979), 201.

4 Caraman, *Saint Angela*, 15.

5 Caraman, *Saint Angela*, 16.

6 Teresa Ledochowska, *Angela Merici and the Company of St. Ursula*, vol. 1 (Rome: Ancora, 1967), 16; Caraman, *Saint Angela*, 26.

7 *Butler's Lives of the Saints*, January, 186.

8 Caraman, *Saint Angela*, 77.

9 Marie Seynaeve, *New Lights on Angela Merici and Her Work* (manuscript, no date), 57.

10 Caraman, *Saint Angela*, 139.

11 "Primitive Rule of St. Angela," 2, in Ledochowska, *Angela Merici and the Company of St. Ursula*, vol. 1, 278.

12 M. Monica, *Angela Merici and Her Teaching Idea* (New York: Longmans, Green and Co., 1927), 163.

13 *Butler's Lives of the Saints*, January, 187.

14 Monica, *Angela Merici and Her Teaching Idea*, 309.

15 Angela Merici left a series of counsels to guide and encourage local leaders of the community. This quotation is from Counsel 5, reproduced in Ledochowska, *Angela Merici and the Company of St. Ursula*, vol. 1, 248.

16 Pope Francis, *The Joy of the Gospel*, 177.

SEVEN Social Justice: Saint Roque González (pp. 98–111)

1 James R. Brockman, *The Word Remains: A Life of Oscar Romero* (Maryknoll, NY: Orbis, 1982), 216.

2 Robert Ellsberg, *All Saints* (New York: Crossroad, 2001), 307.

3 C. J. McNaspy and J. M. Blanch, *Lost Cities of Paraguay* (Chicago: Loyola University Press, 1982), 9.

4 C. J. McNaspy, *Conquistador Without a Sword: The Life of Roque González, S.J.* (Chicago: Loyola Press, 1984), 51.

5 McNaspy, *Conquistador*, 53.

6 In McNaspy, *Conquistador*, 93–95.

7 *Butler's Lives of the Saints*, November, 126.

8 McNaspy, *Conquistador*, 197.

9 McNaspy, *Conquistador*, 204.

10 McNaspy, *Conquistador*, 107.

11 McNaspy and Blanch, 10.

12 *Butler's Lives of the Saints*, November, 126.

13 Pope Francis, General Audience, October 12, 2016.

EIGHT Evangelization: Pope Saint John Paul II (pp. 112–29)

1 Vatican Council II, *Apostolicam Actuositatem,* Decree on the Apostolate of the Laity, 3.

2 Pope Francis, General Audience, October 12, 2016. See, for example, Pope Paul VI, Apostolic Exhortation, *Evangelii Nuntiandi* (On Evangelization in the Modern World), and Pope John Paul II, Encyclical Letter, *Redemptoris Missio* (The Mission of the Redeemer), at http//www.vatican.va.

3 Pope Francis, *The Joy of the Gospel,* 120.

4 Pope John Paul II, Apostolic Exhortation, *Christifideles Laici* (On the Vocation and Mission of the Lay Faithful), 33, at http//www.vatican.va.

5 Pope John Paul II, *Christifideles Laici,* 34.

6 Pope John Paul II, *Christifideles Laici,* 34 (emphasis in the original).

7 Adapted from Pope John Paul II, *Christifideles Laici,* 44.

8 See Pope John Paul II, *Redemptoris Missio.*

9 Pope John Paul II, *Christifideles Laici,* 35.

10 Pope John Paul II, *Ad Limina* visit of the bishops of Southern Germany, December 4, 1992, cited in Avery Dulles, "John Paul II and the New Evangelization: What Does It Mean," in Ralph Martin and Peter Williamson, *John Paul II and the New Evangelization* (Cincinnati, OH: Servant Books, 2006), 13.

11 Pope John Paul II, Message for the Annual World Day of Prayer for Vocations (*I discepoli;* November 1, 1991), in *The Pope Speaks (*vol. 37, no. 3; May/June 1992), 131.

12 George Weigel, *Witness to Hope: The Biography of Pope John Paul II* (New York: Harper Perennial, 2005).

13 150 Weigel, *Witness to Hope,* 350–51.

14 Weigel, *Witness to Hope,* 104.

15 Weigel, *Witness to Hope,* 493.

16 Weigel, *Witness to Hope,* 750.

17 Message of Pope John Paul II for the ninth and tenth World Youth days at http//www .vatican.va (emphasis in the original).

18 Carl Bernstein and Marco Politi, *His Holiness: John Paul II and the Hidden History of Our Time* (Thorndike, ME: Thorndike Press, 1997), 431.

19 Bernstein and Polity, *His Holiness,* 432.

20 Weigel, *Witness to Hope,* 414.

21 Bernstein and Polity, *His Holiness,* 433.

22 Weigel, *Witness to Hope,* 413.

23 Weigel, *Witness to Hope,* 440.

24 Weigel, *Witness to Hope,* 293.

25 Weigel, *Witness to Hope,* 293.

26 Weigel, *Witness to Hope,* 308.

27 Bernstein and Polity, *His Holiness,* 323.

28 Weigel, *Witness to Hope,* 295.

29 Weigel, *Witness to Hope,* 317.

30 Cited in Weigel, *Witness to Hope,* 319–20.

31 Jack Wintz, OFM, "Pope John Paul II and Suffering," at www.Franciscanmeida.org (consulted July 6, 2018).

32 Pope Francis, *Rejoice and Be Glad,* 130.

NINE Perseverance: Saint Jane de Chantal (pp. 130–44)

1 André Ravier, *Saint Jeanne de Chantal: Noble Lady, Holy Woman* (San Francisco: Ignatius Press, 1989), 56.

2 Elisabeth Stopp, *Madame de Chantal* (Westminster, MD: The Newman Press, 1963), 75.

3 Ravier, *Saint Jeanne de Chantal,* 56–57.

4 Mother Françoise-Madeleine de Chaugy, in Ravier, *Saint Jeanne de Chantal,* 62.

5 Ravier, *Saint Jeanne de Chantal,* 74.

6 In Louise Perrotta, ed., *Live Jesus? Wisdom from Saint Francis de Sales and Jane de Chantal* (Frederick, MD: The Word Among Us Press, 2000), 36.

7 In Ravier, *Saint Jeanne de Chantal,* 185–87.

8 *Life and Select Writings of Louis-Marie Grignon de Montfort* (London: Thomas Richardson and Son, 1870), 351.

9 Pope Francis, Homily, April 2, 2017.

TEN Joy: Blessed Pier Giorgio Frassati (pp. 145–59)

1 Luciana Frassati, *A Man of the Beatitudes: Pier Giorgio Frassati* (San Francisco: Ignatius Press, 2001), 68. The picture appears on page 122.

2 The picture appears in the center section of Maria Di Lorenzo, *Blessed Pier Giorgio Frassati: An Ordinary Christian,* trans. Robert Ventresca (Boston: Pauline Books & Media, 2004).

3 Quoted in Bert Ghezzi, *Voices of the Saints: A Year of Readings* (New York: Doubleday, 2000), 612.

4 Adapted from Frassati, *A Man of the Beatitudes,* 39–40.

5 Frassati, *A Man of the Beatitudes,* 43.

6 Frassati, *A Man of the Beatitudes,* 30–31.

7 Frassati, *A Man of the Beatitudes,* 44.

8 Ghezzi, *Voices of the Saints,* 612.

9 Robert Claude, *The Soul of Pier Giorgio Frassati,* trans. Una Morrissy (New York: Spiritual Book Associates, 1960), 16–17.

10 Claude, *The Soul of Pier Giorgio Frassati,* 35–36.

11 Di Lorenzo, *Blessed Pier Giorgio Frassati,* 70.

12 Di Lorenzo, *Blessed Pier Giorgio Frassati,* 73.

13 Di Lorenzo, *Blessed Pier Giorgio Frassati,* 59–60.

14 Di Lorenzo, *Blessed Pier Giorgio Frassati,* p. 57.

15 Di Lorenzo, *Blessed Pier Giorgio Frassati,* 61–62.

16 Adapted from the prayer quoted in Di Lorenzo, *Blessed Pier Giorgio Frassati,* 54.

17 Frassati, *A Man of the Beatitudes,* 40.

18 Frassati, *A Man of the Beatitudes,* 55.

19 Frassati, *A Man of the Beatitudes,* 92.

20 Frassati, *A Man of the Beatitudes,* 25.

21 Frassati, *A Man of the Beatitudes,* 31.

22 Frassati, *A Man of the Beatitudes,* 75–76.

23 Frassati, *A Man of the Beatitudes,* 85.

24 Frassati, *A Man of the Beatitudes,* 86.

25 Frassati, *A Man of the Beatitudes,* 57.

26 Frassati, *A Man of the Beatitudes,* 103–4; Claude, *The Soul of Pier Giorgio Frassati,* 97–98.

27 Frassati, *A Man of the Beatitudes,* 74.

28 Di Lorenzo, *Blessed Pier Giorgio Frassati,* 91.

29 Frassati, *A Man of the Beatitudes,* p. 151.

30 Di Lorenzo, *Blessed Pier Giorgio Frassati,* 102.

31 In Frassati, *A Man of the Beatitudes,* 164 and 166.

32 Pope Francis, Homily, May 23, 2016.

Bibliography

Aelred of Rievaulx, *The Mirror of Charity.* Translated by Elizabeth Connor with an introduction by Charles Dumont. Kalamazoo, MI: Cistercian Publications, 1990.

Aelred of Rievaulx, *Spiritual Friendship.* Cistercian Fathers Series 5. Translated by Mary Eugenia Laker with an introduction by Douglass Roby. Kalmazoo, MI: Cistercian Publications, 1977.

Allaire, James and Rosemary Brougton. *Praying with Dorothy Day.* Winona, MN: Saint Mary's Press, 1995. [Currently owned and distributed by The Word Among Us Press, Frederick, Maryland.]

The Autobiography of Saint Thérèse of Lisieux: The Story of a Soul. Translated by John Beevers. New York: Doubleday Image Books, 1989.

Beevers, John. *Saint Thérèse, the Little Flower: The Making of a Saint.* Rockford, IL: Tan Books and Publishers, 1976.

Bernstein, Carl, and Marco Politi. *His Holiness: John Paul II and the Hidden History of Our Time.* Thorndike, ME: Thorndike Press, 1997.

Bouyer, Louis. *The Cistercian Heritage.* Westminster, MD: The Newman Press, 1958.

Brockman, James R. *The Word Remains: A Life of Oscar Romero.* Maryknoll, NY: Orbis Books, 1982.

Brodrick, James. *A Procession of Saints.* New York: Longmans, Green and Co., 1949.

Caraman, Philip. *Saint Angela: The Life of Angela Merici, Foundress of the Ursulines.* New York: Farrar, Straus and Company, 1963.

Claude, Robert. *The Soul of Pier-Giorgio Frassati.* Translated by Una Morrissy. New York: Spiritual Book Associates, 1960.

Daniel, Walter. *The Life of Ailred of Rievaulx.* Translated with an introduction by F. M. Powicke. London: Thomas Nelson and Sons, 1950.

David, Charles, ed. *English Spiritual Writers.* New York: Sheed & Ward, 1961.

Day, Dorothy. *The Long Loneliness.* Garden City, NJ: Image Books, 1959.

Denier, Dom Paul. "St. Ailred of Rievaulx." In David Hugh Farmer, ed. *Benedict's Disciples.* Leominster, Herefordshire: Fowler Wright Books, Ltd., 1980.

De Sales, St. Francis. *Introduction to the Devout Life.* Translated by John K. Ryan. New York: Image Books, 1989.

Di Lorenzo, Maria. *Blessed Pier Giorgio Frassati: An Ordinary Christian.* Translated by Robert Ventresca. Boston: Pauline Books & Media, 2004.

Duffy, Consuela Marie. *Katharine Drexel: A Biography.* Bethlehem, PA: Mother Katharine Drexel Guild, 1987.

Ellsberg, Robert. *All Saints.* New York: Crossroad, 2001.

Englebert, Omer. *St. Francis of Assisi: A Biography.* Ann Arbor, MI: Servant Books, 1979.

Frassati, Luciana. *A Man of the Beatitudes: Pier Giorgio Frassati.* San Francisco: Ignatius Press, 2001.

Ghezzi, Bert. *Voices of the Saints: A Year of Readings.* New York: Doubleday, 2000.

Holt, Mary van Balen. *Meet Katharine Drexel.* Ann Arbor, MI: Servant Publications, 2002.

Jörgensen, Johannes. *St. Francis of Assisi: A Biography.* Garden City, NJ: Image Books, 1955.

Kempis, Thomas à. *The Imitation of Christ.* Translated by Richard Whitford and edited by Harold Gardiner. New York: Image Books, 1989.

Ledochowska, Teresa. *Angela Merici and the Company of St. Ursula.* Vol. 2, *An Educator and Apostle of the Pre-Tridentine Reform.* Rome: Ancora, 1967.

Letters of Saint Frances Xavier Cabrini. Translated by Ursula Infante. Milan: Ancora, 1970

The Letters of John Baptist de La Salle. Translated by Colman Molloy. Romeoville, IL: Lasallian Publications, 1988.

Martin, Ralph, and Peter Williamson, eds. *John Paul II and the New Evangelization.* Cincinnati: Servant Books, 2006.

Marty, Martin E., "Dorothy Day: The Exemplar." In Paul Elie, ed. *A Tremor of Bliss: Contemporary Writers on the Saints.* New York: Harcourt Brace & Company, 1994.

McNaspy, C. J. *Conquistador Without a Sword: The Life of Roque González, S.J.* Chicago: Loyola Press, 1984.

McNaspy, C. J., and J. M. Blanch. *Lost Cities of Paraguay.* Chicago: Loyola University Press, 1982.

Merriman, Brigid O'Shea. *Searching for Christ: The Spirituality of Dorothy Day.* Notre Dame, IN: University of Notre Dame Press, 1994.

Mitchell, Patricia, ed. *A Radical Love: Wisdom from Dorothy Day.* Ijamsville, MD: The Word Among Us Press, 2000.

Monica, M. *Angela Merici and Her Teaching Idea.* New York: Longmans, Green and Co., 1927.

Noonan, Peggy. *John Paul the Great: Remembering a Spiritual Father.* New York: Viking Penguin, 2005.

Perrotta, Louise, ed. *Live Jesus! Wisdom from Saints Francis de Sales and Jane de Chantal.* Ijamsville, MD: The Word Among Us Press, 2000.

Ravier, André. *Saint Jeanne de Chantal: Noble Lady, Holy Woman.* San Francisco: Ignatius Press, 1989.

Riegle, Rosalie G. *Dorothy Day: Portraits by Those Who Knew Her.* Maryknoll, NY: Orbis Books, 2003.

Schmidt, Joseph F. *Praying with Thérèse of Lisieux.* Frederick, MD: The Word Among Us Press, 1991.

Seelos, Francis Xavier. "Sermons." Redemptorist Archives, Baltimore Province (RABP), III, 21; 228 and 230.

Seynaeve, Marie. *New Lights on Angela Merici and Her Work.* Translated by Anne Benyon. Manuscript, n.d.

Squire, Aelred. *Aelred of Rievaulx: A Study.* London: SPCK, 1973.

Stopp, Elisabeth. *Madame de Chantal.* Westminster, MD: The Newman Press, 1963.

Tylenda, Joseph N. *Jesuit Saints & Martyrs,* 2nd ed. Chicago: Loyola Press, 1998.

Weigel, George. *Witness to Hope: The Biography of Pope John Paul II.* New York: Harper Perennial, 2005.

Wright, Wendy M., and Joseph F. Power, eds. *Francis de Sales, Jane de Chantal: Letters of Spitritual Direction. The Classics of Western Spirituality.* New York: Paulist Press.

Zwick, Mark and Louise, "Dorothy Day and the Catholic Worker Movement." In Dorothy Day, *On Pilgrimage,* 1–64. Grand Rapids, MI: Wm. B. Eerdmans, 1999.

Acknowledgments

Thanks to the following colleagues and friends who contributed to this book with their prayers, wisdom, and expertise: Donald Cooper, Joseph Durepos, Richard Easton, Donald Fishel, Kelly Hughes, Henry Libersat, Mary Lothschutz, Patty Mitchell, Margaret Procario, Chris Rush, Jeff Smith, and William G. Storey.

I am grateful to Jon Sweeney, Robert Edmonson, and everyone at Paraclete Press for their enthusiastic, energetic, and excellent publication of *Saints at Heart*.

And a special word of thanks to my readers and to the booksellers and distributors who make my books available.

About Paraclete Press

Who We Are

As the publishing arm of the Community of Jesus, Paraclete Press presents a full expression of Christian belief and practice—from Catholic to Evangelical, from Protestant to Orthodox, reflecting the ecumenical charism of the Community and its dedication to sacred music, the fine arts, and the written word. We publish books, recordings, sheet music, and video/DVDs that nourish the vibrant life of the church and its people.

What We Are Doing

Books | PARACLETE PRESS BOOKS show the richness and depth of what it means to be Christian. While Benedictine spirituality is at the heart of who we are and all that we do, our books reflect the Christian experience across many cultures, time periods, and houses of worship.

We have many series, including *Paraclete Essentials*; *Paraclete Fiction*; *Paraclete Poetry*; *Paraclete Giants*; and for children and adults, *All God's Creatures*, books about animals and faith; and *San Damiano Books*, focusing on Franciscan spirituality. Others include *Voices from the Monastery* (men and women monastics writing about living a spiritual life today), *Active Prayer*, and new for young readers: *The Pope's Cat*. We also specialize in gift books for children on the occasions of Baptism and First Communion, as well as other important times in a child's life, and books that bring creativity and liveliness to any adult spiritual life.

The MOUNT TABOR BOOKS series focuses on the arts and literature as well as liturgical worship and spirituality; it was created in conjunction with the Mount Tabor Ecumenical Centre for Art and Spirituality in Barga, Italy.

Music | The PARACLETE RECORDINGS label represents the internationally acclaimed choir *Gloriæ Dei Cantores*, the *Gloriæ Dei Cantores Schola*, and the other instrumental artists of the *Arts Empowering Life Foundation*.

Paraclete Press is the exclusive North American distributor for the Gregorian chant recordings from St. Peter's Abbey in Solesmes, France. Paraclete also carries all of the Solesmes chant publications for Mass and the Divine Office, as well as their academic research publications.

In addition, PARACLETE PRESS SHEET MUSIC publishes the work of today's finest composers of sacred choral music, annually reviewing over 1,000 works and releasing between 40 and 60 works for both choir and organ.

Video | Our video/DVDs offer spiritual help, healing, and biblical guidance for a broad range of life issues including grief and loss, marriage, forgiveness, facing death, understanding suicide, bullying, addictions, Alzheimer's, and Christian formation.

Learn more about us at our website:
www.paracletepress.com
or phone us toll-free at 1.800.451.5006

SCAN TO
READ
MORE

You may also be interested in . . .

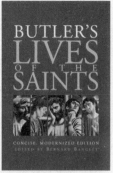

Butler's Lives of the Saints
Concise, Modernized Edition
Edited by Bernard Bangley
ISBN 978-1-55725-422-1 | Trade Paperback | $27.99

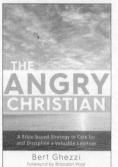

My Year with the Saints for Kids
Compiled by Peter Celano
ISBN 978-1-64060-167-3 | Trade Paperback | $14.99

The Angry Christian
Bert Ghezzi,
Foreword by Brandon Vogt
ISBN 978-1-64060-039-3 | Hardcover | $19.99